# BLACK CAESAR

## THE RISE AND DISAPPEARANCE
## OF FRANK MATTHEWS, KINGPIN

RON CHEPESIUK

13-digit ISBN 978-0-9852440-1-9
10-digit ISBN 0-9852440-1-1

# CONTENTS

# FOREWORD

IN THE 1970s the heroin market in the United States was dominated by a black distributor named Frank Matthews who operated out of New York. He was the most notable black figure on the East Coast at the time and one of the first major independents who challenged La Cosa Nostra for supremacy in the criminal underworld. Black Caesar, as he was known, was a new kind of super criminal ruling a nationwide empire of dope. He was the boss of bosses, and the DEA ranks him as one of the Top Ten drug traffickers in United States history.

A pivotal figure in the history of the drug trade, Matthews was one of the nation's largest narcotics dealers from the 1960s through the early 1970s, and he routinely handled multi-million dollar shipments. More importantly, Matthews was the first black man astute and confident enough to control an interstate organization the size and scope of his operation at a time when the Mob controlled everything, illegal or otherwise. Remarkably, Frank Matthews did it while still in his twenties.

He became a major dealer in twenty-one states with quality overseas contacts for both heroin and cocaine. Frank was a North Carolina country boy who seized control of the black rackets in New York City. The DEA said that Matthews imported heroin from Turkey by way of processing plants in Marseilles, France and cocaine from Latin America. Street legend has it that his wealth could not be counted.

Indeed, Black Caesar had Pablo Escobar-type money in the early 1970s; yet, it didn't go to his head. To Matthews money was nothing but a thing. He controlled the illegal drug market in the inner-cities from the East Coast to the West Coast and had contacts with Cuban wholesalers who controlled vast portions of the South American coke trade to the United States. Matthews earned respect in the streets and criminal underworld by holding his own against the Mafia. When his profits became so huge that they took notice he did not bow down, he dictated. In essence, Frank was the first black man that shook and unsettled the Mob. He was a true trend setter and set the standard for future street legends who followed in his path and tried to earn the title of "Kingpin".

Matthews was Mr. Big. In four years he made an estimated 300 million, and by the early 1970s, Matthews' organization was handling multimillion dollar shipments in 21 states. His well-oiled and profitable operation functioned like a machine. He worked on strict business principles—high grade heroin sold at fair prices with a ruthless attitude toward payment. Dealers could cut Frank's coke ten times and put an eighty on the heroin. Frank would descend on a town in his Cadillac and give local distributors the benefit of his wisdom. He franchised like McDonald's.

A suitable candidate for a Matthews' dealership would be identified in advance by one of several point men Frank employed to find market opportunities for him, and it was almost always an agreeable experience. At his height of power, Matthews probably accounted for the distribution of about one third of all the heroin entering the country. His purchasing power was the kind the Corsicans could not ignore and the deals he brokered showed his stature.

Matthews spent his time with wine, women, coke and gambling. Staying in luxury hotels and driving cars like his gold Lincoln Mark III, working his magic on hustlers across the United States to sell his dope. Matthews was suspected by the feds of trafficking heroin in seven or eight regions of the country. He was a marketing expert who flaunted his wealth. He would appear in all his glory in a full length black sable coat or a black leather safari suit, driving yet another brand new El Dorado to hit the Persian Room on a Saturday night.

He used to tell people, "You know how it is when you got a hundred thousand things on your mind? The bigger you are in drugs, the more careful you got to be to stay clean. You got to keep away from the stuff. You got to stay off the streets and you got to line other people up to take the fall when there is trouble." But Frank did not follow his own advice. He was right down there in the mix. Doing everything he did not need to be doing and getting his hands dirty. Frank used cocaine, melting it with smack to make speedballs. Despite his status, Black Caesar reportedly never carried a gun. His presence was intimidating enough.

Matthews loved cocaine too. It was not just his business, it was his breakfast, lunch and dinner, a complete life support system. He was Tony Montana come to life—the black scarface. He seemed possessed by a sense of invincibility and a godlike mastery over his own fate.

To dudes in the streets Matthews is a hero, an outlaw of epic proportions, the hustler who did it his way and got away with it. He gave the United States government the big fuck you and blatantly defied them right to their face. He bypassed the Mob, the preeminent criminal structure of the day, by importing his heroin directly through Venezuela from Turkey by way of processing plants in Marseilles, France. He got his cocaine straight from Latin American long before the Colombian cocaine cartels were in vogue. Locally he eliminated the middleman by handling the narcotics all the way down to the street sales, plus sold weight to big dealers in other cities. He was the original American Gangster- fuck all that other shit- Frank Matthews was the real deal and god's honest truth when it came to this gangster shit. He did it in the dope game like no one else, before or after him.

In this book, gangster writer Ron Chepesiuk examines every detail, myth and legend of the Frank Matthews folklore in one mesmerizing, intriguing and concise volume. It is both the story of one of the biggest legends in organized crime history and the longest manhunts in U.S. law enforcement history. Through Ron Chepesiuk's research and writing we come to understand better the complex and fascinating character that Frank Matthews was.

—Seth Ferranti, author of *Rayful Edmond: Washington DC's Most Notorious Drug Lord*, *The Supreme Team: The Birth of Crack and Hip-Hop*, Prince's Reign of Terror *and the Supreme/50 Cent Beef Exposed*, *Gorilla Convict: The Prison Writings of Seth Ferranti* and *Prison Stories and Street Legends Vol. 1 and 2*.

# JUMPING BAIL

*"Mr. Deary, am I going to get that life count they've been talking about?"*
Frank Matthews

**J**ULY 2, 1973—a typical hot, muggy day in New York City. Frank Matthews, alleged drug kingpin, is scheduled to appear in a federal court in Brooklyn, New York. He is already facing six charges of drug trafficking and conspiracy, but the new indictment will add charges and supersede the first one. On December 20, 1972, federal prosecutors swore out a warrant for Matthews' arrest, accusing him of possessing 15 kilos of cocaine worth an estimated $3.6 million at street prices. About two weeks later, the authorities finally arrested Matthews in Las Vegas, one of his favorite haunts, as he prepared to leave the city and fly to Los Angeles for the Super Bowl VII game between the Miami Dolphins and Washington Redskins.

After being extradited from Las Vegas to New York City, Matthews had managed to secure bail despite the claim of the federal government that he is the U.S.'s biggest drug trafficker. Federal prosecutors and law enforcement officials who investigated the Matthews organization considered the bail of $325,000 a bad joke, and they worried that Matthews would skip town. After all, investigators had evidence that Matthews may be been quietly stashing $1 million a month for the past several months. So why, they wondered, would the drug kingpin be doing that unless he was preparing for his imminent flight? All Matthews had to do to meet the bond requirements was to report regularly to the U.S. Attorney's office and stay within the jurisdiction of the Eastern District of New York. Being short of manpower, law enforcement had no way of keeping tabs on Matthews.

The suspect's attitude and demeanor reinforced the authorities' concern. The charismatic and handsome Matthews swaggered into the federal courthouse and greeting everyone he met with a broad smile and a friendly nod, while flirting with the ladies. Law enforcement officials could only look on and marvel. "Frank looked and acted like the King of New York City," said Ray Deary, the Assistant United States Attorney for the Eastern District who had served in the Appeals Division since 1971. "He walked around our turf like he owned it."

Deary was right. Frank Matthews is no ordinary criminal. On the mean streets of the urban jungles of America Matthews' exploits have earned him the moniker of "Black Caesar." He is charismatic as well as dangerous and even his adversaries, the authorities, have a grudging respect for him.

Matthews seemingly unconcern about the serious charges that could put him in jail for several decades baffled the authorities. They could not tail him, but they had received reports that Matthews has been conducting business with his associates even before securing bail. Sources within the West Street Detention Center, where Matthews had been detained after his arrest, observed that top lieutenants of his organization, as well as his lawyer, Gino Gallina, were visiting him frequently, and it seemed to the sources that Matthews was giving instructions and orders.

After his release on bond, Black Caesar was seen in the company of several leading drug dealers and gamblers. Moreover, Matthews was in the constant company of Cheryl Denise Brown, a beautiful light-skinned black woman who turned heads wherever she went. It should have been an embarrassment to the alleged drug kingpin since he had a common law wife, Barbara Hinton, and three kids waiting for him at home. But Hinton, herself an attractive woman, did not seem to be bothered or embarrassed by Matthews' apparent public infidelity, even after the family was forced to leave their luxurious surroundings for a more modest apartment at 2785 Ocean Parkway in Brooklyn. In better days, Matthews had used the Ocean Parkway apartment as a getaway and a place to stash his many paramours. In their effort to nail Matthews, prosecutors hauled Hinton before a grand jury, offering her immunity if she would cooperate with their case against her husband. Hinton refused, even though she faced a possible conspiracy charge herself.

Then a few days before his scheduled court appearance, Matthews arrived in the Brooklyn federal court building with his lawyer, Gino Gallina, when he bumped into Federal Prosecutor Raymond Deary as Deary was leaving a room. Matthews said to Deary, "Mr. Deary, am I gonna get that life count they been talking about?" Matthews was referring to part of section 848 of the Controlled Substances Act of 1970: "Any person who engages in a continuing criminal enterprise shall be sentenced to a term of imprisonment which may not be less than 20 years and which may be up to life imprisonment." The thought of Section 848 terrified many traffickers because they feared that, if convicted under the statue, they would spend the rest of their lives in prison.

Deary looked at Matthews and said, "It's very possible, Frank…very possible." Later, Deary said he was joking, but for Matthews, spending his life in jail was no joking matter. "Frank knew what the 848 could do to him," recalled Liddy Jones, a former drug kingpin and an associate of Matthews. "No way was he going to spend the rest of his life in jail."

Inside the steamy courthouse on this sweltering July day in 1973, the electric fans whirred as the judge, federal prosecutors and the defense team waited patiently for Frank Matthews to appear. But he never did. Instead, he became a fugitive from justice. In the coming weeks, the U.S. Drug Enforcement Administration (DEA), the lead agency in the investigation of Frank Matthews, is confident they will apprehend the fugitive. After all, don't law enforcement officials always get their man? The weeks turned into months and the months into years, and law enforcement did not catch him. The U.S. Marshal Service took over the hunt for

Matthews from the DEA. There were alleged sightings of Matthews in more than 50 countries. Cheryl Brown, Matthews' mistress disappeared the same time he did, and her whereabouts were just as mysterious. No informant stepped forward. No bodies were ever found. No fingerprints were discovered. No solid leads appeared. Nothing.

With time, law enforcement moved on to other priorities. New generations of law enforcement officials replaced the old guard and they knew little about Matthews. Periodically, Matthews' story appeared briefly in the press and rekindled speculation. Is he alive or is he dead? The public wondered. But then the reports faded from public consciousness and people focused on other crime stories.

What follows is the remarkable story of the legendary Frank Matthews, one of organized crime's most original gangsters. It is the story of the biggest gangster mystery of all time. It is a story with an improbable beginning and a story with no conclusive ending.

# ONE

# THE FORMATIVE YEARS

*"People brag they knew Frank, but they didn't really know him. You could never really get close to Frank."*
**A Matthews' friend**

**M**ANY ASPECTS OF Frank Larry Matthews' legendary life are shrouded in mystery, but none are more mysterious than the details of his formative years. It is difficult to develop a clear picture of Matthews' early life because of so many conflicting accounts and because many people who knew him in his formative years refuse to talk about him. As Ricky Johnson, a native of Durham, North Carolina, explained, "You hear so many stories about Frank Matthews. It's hard to distinguish what's what. They all have a different version of growing up with him. You realize a lot of what you hear is really just rumor." Another Durham source said, "A lot of people like to make up stories so they can be in the limelight. They say they ran with Frank, sold drugs for him, but then you realize they are younger than Matthews and not from the same generation. They just want to be a part of the legend."

Frank Matthews, in many ways, remains a closely guarded city secret in Durham. As one Durham native who knew Matthews said, "You ain't going to get people from here to open up about Pee Wee. They are either thinking you with the law or they fear they may say something that can come back and bite em." Or as J.C. Skippy Scarborough, owner of the Scarborough and Hargett Funeral Home in Durham, candidly explained: "People here are cautious. Many think Pee Wee Matthews is still alive. You never know who is listening or what may get back to him."

What is crystal clear about Frank Matthews, though, is that the remarkable and dynamic environment he grew up in helped to shape his life in a way that made him one of the biggest gangsters of all time. Birth records show that Matthews was born on February 13, 1944, but where he was born and maybe to whom is still unclear. Frank's father and mother are believed to be Arthur and Hazel McNeal Matthews, and it is certain that Frank was raised by his aunt, Marzella Steele Webb, after Frank's mother died. Most reports say Frank Matthews was four years old when his mother died, but her death certificate indicates she actually died on November 20, 1953, when Frank was nine years old.

Sources describe Marzella as an attractive, business-like and community oriented woman who looked a lot like her nephew Frank. Some people in tight-lipped Durham maintain or speculate that Marzella could be the young boy's mother. Some also say that Frank's mother came from Mississippi where Frank may have been born. What is surprising is how little information people in Durham have about one of their most famous sons. In any case, Marzella took Frank in and raised the young boy like he was her son, even though she had two young children of her own to support.

Matthews was born and raised in the segregated era in the East End of north Durham in the heart of North Carolina tobacco country. Today, Durham, the fifth largest city in the state, can attribute its growth to the establishment of the tobacco industry by magnate Washington Duke and his sons. By the early twentieth century, the Dukes had established a virtual monopoly on smoking and chewing tobacco products in the U.S. Washington Duke eventually became a philanthropist, and among his major accomplishments was the founding of Duke University in East Durham. Still, strip away the veneer of respectability, and history shows that the Dukes were true robber barons in the mold of Andrew Carnegie and John D. Rockefeller. Durham grew as a tobacco town in which blacks, although comprising the majority of the city's population, occupied the bottom rung of the economic ladder.

The East End has largely been African American since its inception in the late 1890s. Some residents from Matthews' neighborhood were lucky to find work in the textile mills that grew in number outside Durham, but most did not. In the late 1940s Durham began its economic slide downwards, and African Americans bore the brunt of that slide. Between 1957 and 1959 employment in the manufacturing sector in Durham dropped 19 percent while the weekly wages were a measly $64.61. Statistics show that by the 1950s over half of the local black labor force consisted of unskilled workers and service or domestic workers employed by whites. Clearly, there wasn't much opportunity for ambitious young blacks in Durham during that period.

With segregation a stark reality, Durham's black community turned inward early in its history and developed a vibrant, self-sufficient community. In the words of J.C. Scarborough, Durham is "rich in black history." It is an obvious fact that this had a huge impact on young Frank Matthews. The center of this dynamic black community was Hayti, an area located just south of the town center. Indeed, Hayti can lay claim to being the country's first self-sufficient African American community. "Durham was as segregated as any city in the country, but even though there was poverty, Durham's black community prospered," explained Andre Vann, a local historian and archivist at the Durham-based North Carolina Central University "As early as 1910, Booker T. Washington described Durham as "a city of Negro enterprise" and said that "of all cities in the country, Durham was the one most amicable in terms of black-white relations."

Scarborough pointed out, "Durham didn't have the lynchings and violence against blacks that so many other places in the South experienced." Wayne Watson, a police officer in Durham in the 1960s, described how he viewed black-white relations at the time: "Being an old country (white) boy, I thought race relations were good. A lot of blacks in Durham had money."

Durham's Parish Street became known as "The Black Wall Street," and among its notable businesses were the North Carolina Mutual Life Insurance Company, the nation's oldest and largest black-owned insurance company, and M and F Bank, one of the country's oldest African-American owned banks. North Carolina Central University, founded in 1910 to train African American Sunday school teachers, was the country's first publicly supported liberal arts college for African-Americans. The Hayti District, where all classes of blacks lived, not only had its own businesses but also its own schools, churches, library, theaters, hotels, a hospital and other services.

Charles Clinton, a Durham native and Matthews' friend, recalled, "Durham in segregation days had everything a black person could want. We had a lot of black wealth. Per capita, we had more black millionaires than any city in North Carolina. So blacks could find ways to earn money." By the 1950s the country was changing in terms of race relations, and according to Clinton, "The atmosphere of this period gave young blacks the incentive to try to achieve more."

Although from the poor side of town, Matthews could not help but be affected in a positive way by black Durham's environment of distinction. And despite the hard economic times for blacks in the 1950s and 1960s, he saw plenty of examples of successful black entrepreneurs who had overcome the obstacles of race and economics.

"Durham, North Carolina was a unique place, and one of the capitals of black entrepreneurship in the country," explained Al Bradley, co-director of the award-winning documentary, *The Frank Matthews Story*. "Matthews must have seen lots of black owned businesses and successful black men while he was growing up. That later gave him the chutzpah to circumvent the Italian mafia in the drug business. That was unheard of at the time. Something in Matthews' growing up gave him the confidence to stride fearlessly into a world that didn't respect him."

Today in Durham, Matthews is still known as "Pee Wee." The nickname stuck to him into his adult years, even though he grew up to be a full-sized, about 5'8" and 180 pounds, well built, and exceptionally strong man. It seemed everybody who knew Pee Wee as a youngster had a fond memory of the legend. One source who grew up with Pee Wee claimed, "He could run faster than a cheetah. You could never catch him." Many who knew Matthews say he had a distinctive high pitched voice, although some say his voice would only reach a high pitch when he was excited or agitated.

He attended both the East End grade school, the third oldest grade school for African- Americans organized in North Carolina, and Whitted Junior High School, before entering Hillside High School. Locals who went to school with Pee Wee said that even at a young age Pee Wee was unselfish and very generous in spirit. A woman who said she took machine shop in high school with Matthews recalled how she never saw Pee Wee without money.

In segregation days, black Durham was also known as the "Harlem of the South" for the way the city attracted top notch black entertainment. Durham became part of the famous Chitlin Circuit, the collective name given to the string of performance venues throughout the eastern and southern United States that allowed African American musicians to perform in the era of segregation. The Chitlin Circuit operated from the early 19th century through the 1960s and featured entertainers as diverse as Redd Foxx, Moms Mabley, Cab Calloway, Ella Fitzgerald and Duke Ellington. Younger entertainers, such as James Brown, Jimi Hendrix, Little Richard, Smokey Robinson and Chuck Berry, who became stars of the new musical genre, Rock and Roll, and toured the Chitlin Circuit, became the heroes of many young black men in Durham during the 1950s.

Pee Wee Matthews, however, was a huge fan of Clyde McPhatter, a second tier entertainer and Durham native. McPhatter had grown up in the same part of Durham as Pee Wee, and he showed what a young man from Durham could do if he was willing to leave home and seek his fortune. McPhatter, best known for his solo hit "A Lover's Question," was a high pitched tenor who, in his brief life (1932-1972), played a big role in shaping Rhythm and Blues and Do Wop music. The entertainer returned a few times to his old neighborhood to show off the trappings of his success—a new Cadillac, a roll of money, sharp clothes and expensive jewelry. Clyde McPhatter undoubtedly made an impression on young Pee Wee.

After making it as a big-time drug dealer in the late 1960s, Pee Wee would also return to his native Durham to show off the spoils of success. "The police often knew Matthews was in town because it was big news," revealed Wayne Watson, a retired Durham City police officer.

Today, Matthews' big splash visits to the city are still recalled. "I came back with Pee Wee in the late 1960s," recalled RB, one of Matthews' boyhood friends. "We were doing good. We drove down in our El Eldorados, wearing top of the line tailored suits…looking cool. We really impressed our homeboys."

Like many of the homeboys who grew up with Matthews, RB would stay in touch with him, even after Matthews became busy as a drug dealer in New York City. "If I went to New York City, I didn't have to tell Frank. He knew about it," RB explained. "He would make a special effort to reach out to me."

When Pee Wee left Durham in search of a better future, he took Durham with him both in spirit and experience. "He was a country boy by heart, but I don't think New York City or the drug game was ready for a ballsy and astute guy like him," said Seth Ferranti, publisher of the *Gorilla Convict* web site and Matthews biographer. "His simple beginnings shaped, prepared and inspired him to become the man he became. To him, the big city must have seemed like a jungle when he arrived, but it was a jungle where he would become king."

RB was not the only one from Durham who came to visit Pee Wee in New York City, but when they did, Matthews loved to impress them. William Babe Cameron, one of Pee Wee's homeboys, described the time Matthews came to visit his friend, hoping to secure a drug deal and make some money. "I'm going to pick up some money, why don't you come along?" Matthews said to Cameron. Making one stop after another, Matthews kept packing shopping bags full of cash in his Thunderbird, filling up the back seat and trunk. Matthews even had to throw out the spare tire to make more room. Cameron was awestruck. He had never seen so many dead presidents in his life. When the car ran out of room, Matthews stopped the pickups, and the two friends returned home to Matthews' apartment in Brooklyn. Matthews then walked into the bedroom and unlocked a big clothes closet. Cameron looked inside and almost keeled over. Bags of money were packed into the closet to a height of at least six feet.

Matthews gave some evidence that he had an ambition early in life to pursue his dreams in the wider world. Roger Garay, a New York Police Department (NYPD) detective assigned to the New York Joint Federal Narcotics Task Force, investigated Matthews in the early 1970s. Garay recalled, "A grade school teacher whom we interviewed later during the course of our Matthews investigation told us that when Pee Wee was about six years of age, he wrote an essay revealing his big dream to travel to South America." Later, when Frank Matthews was a budding kingpin, he would visit Venezuela and use Caracas, its capitol, as the linchpin for smuggling drugs to the U.S.

By the 1950s, race relations in Durham, as in other parts of the country were changing. In 1954 came the momentous U.S. Supreme Court Decision, Brown versus the Board of Education, which ended legal segregation in the public schools. In 1956 Dr. Martin Luther King spoke at Hillside High, at the time one of the southeast's highest academically ranked black high schools. The first sit-in is attributed to the Greensboro, North Carolina students who occupied the Woolworth counter for six months in 1960. But three years before, as Pee Wee Matthews was about to enter Hillside High, the country's first sit-in actually happened in Hayti on June 23, 1957, when a Reverend Douglas E. Moore and six others occupied whites-only booths in the segregated Royal Ice Cream Parlor and refused to move. The manager called the police, and the men who became known as the Royal 7 were arrested and found guilty of trespassing. In the 1959-60 school year, two women became the first black students to enter a white school, Broyden Junior High.

By the time blacks in Durham had gathered for the largest mass demonstration in Durham history on May 17, 1963, Frank Matthews had already left Durham to seek fame and fortune in the big city. We know little about how the young man felt about segregation and race relations, but it is certain that he was proud to be black and resented any kind of white domination. Indeed, Black Caesar was said to be an admirer of Malcolm X. One friend recalled, "One time, Malcolm came on the radio and was giving one of his fiery speeches. I was going to turn the radio down, but Pee Wee said, 'Don't turn it down, man. That's my man, Malcolm.'"

From an early age, Pee Wee showed himself to be s fearless leader of the boys in the neighborhood. "Pee Wee inspired loyalty; kids wanted to follow him," recalled one boyhood friend. Another Matthews friend, nicknamed Tic, "ran" with Pee Wee and attended elementary school with him. Tic described Pee Wee as "mean" and tough. We played a game on the playground called Hot Ball," he recalled with a smile. "Whenever Pee Wee controlled the ball, we had a hard time taking it off of him."

Pee Wee also knew how to think on his feet. "I heard that whenever something memorable happened to Pee Wee, he would say, 'a lesson has been learned,'" Ricky Johnson revealed. "He had the great ability to learn from his experience."

Pee Wee always seemed to be getting into fights, but he knew how to take care of himself. "I got into a fight with him and he busted my lip," Tic said. "We were about the same size but he was two years older than me." One time, however, Pee Wee picked on the wrong person. "There was a girl named Linda Fletcher who hung with us," Tic recalled. "She was a real tomboy. But one time Pee Wee got mad at Linda and hit her in the head with a coke bottle. Linda jumped Pee Wee and started pounding him (laughs). I don't think Pee Wee messed with her again." Tic also commented on Pee Wee's relationship with his Aunt Marzella: "She treated Pee Wee good, like her own son. They were very close."

People who knew Matthews when he was a kid invariably use the same two words to describe him: tough and charismatic. He would remain so later in life when he had to deal with some of the toughest gangsters on the planet: La Cosa Nostra. Matthews would warn the Mob, "Touch any of my men and I'll drive down Mulberry Street (in Brooklyn) and shoot every wop I see."

Tic noted that Pee Wee was not serious about school, but he was street smart. "Even in those days he was always about money," he said. "Pee Wee was a hustler."

RB began hanging around with Pee Wee from about age 11. He remembers Pee Wee Matthews as having a good side and being a person who would help you if he liked you. Pee Wee, RB and some friends liked to go to Marvin Bett's hot dog stand and then to the movies. "Pee Wee was a man of his word, a straight shooter," RB recalled. "He was always hustling. Although he got involved in a lot of petty crime, he never robbed anybody."

Pee Wee seemed good-natured and was obviously charismatic, but his friend Peter Thorp revealed that he always had a reserved, distant side. "People brag that they knew Frank, but they didn't really know him," Thorp said. "You could never really get close to Frank."

Charles Clinton remembered Pee Wee as the type of friend one could count on. He recalled the time Matthews came to his 28th birthday party. "He was quiet and let me be the center of attention. After all, it was my party. You wouldn't even know he was in the room."

One man from Durham recalled the time Pee Wee came by his house in the summer of 1960 and made quite an impression on him. "He was a cocky kid who always looked nicely dressed," he said. "I heard later that Pee Wee liked his women pretty and light skinned and my wife was both. He ogled my wife and in his high-pitched voice said to me, 'Man how did you get a fine looking wife like that. She's sure pretty. She looks almost white.' I told my wife, 'don't you ever let that boy in our house.'"

RB was a year older than Pee Wee, and he recalls his friend as being big and strong like an NFL running back. "Pee Wee was a natural who would fight anybody over anything," RB explained. "You could be 25 pounds heavier than him. It didn't matter." RB and Pee Wee had it out once in front of the school. "We were friends, but he would fight me if he got mad at me," RB said.

RB recalled hopping the train with Pee Wee and some pals and going by the Farmer's Exchange to steal chickens. "One of us would go inside the fence and make the chickens panic and run around. Pee Wee would run them down. He was quick. We boys would catch about four chickens, bring them to the liquor houses and sell them for about a quarter apiece. In those days, you could buy a lot of things with a dollar."

Another story involves a white bootlegger who would deliver liquor for the liquor houses in Pee Wee's neighborhood. When the bootlegger went inside the liquor house to deliver his booze, Pee Wee and some of his friends would sneak into the car and steal some liquor. Occasionally, the white bootlegger would fire shots into the air to scare the thieves off.

Much has been made of Pee Wee's chicken thievery, but his petty crime was not atypical among Durham's black youth. "All of us were involved in some way in a side hustle," Clinton revealed. "A lot of kids, not just Frank, stole chickens from the Farmer's Exchange."

Matthews, though, was not always successful as a petty thief. According to police records, at age 14, Pee Wee was charged with assault and battery and was released in the custody of his aunt Marzella.

Wayne Watson recalled one pleasant Saturday afternoon in the spring of 1961 when the Durham Police Department received a tip that someone was stealing chickens from the Farmer's Exchange. "I went out there with another officer and saw a young black man running back into the woods behind Canal Street. We arrested him for stealing chickens. The boy was Frank Matthews. He admitted to stealing chickens. Pee Wee cooperated, but he looked like he had no fear of us. He was just 16 or 17, so the judge didn't give him any jail time. But he told Pee Wee to stay away from the Farmer's Exchange."

It was not the last time Wayne Watson would hear of Frank Matthews. "A couple of years later, a black man joined the Durham Police Department. He was married to Marzella, Pee Wee's aunt. I was the man's sergeant, and we worked the midnight shift. He told me he wanted certain Saturdays off so he could go to New York City. I gave him the okay. He would get back from New York late Saturday and would often be late for work. He apologized and explained that he went to see his nephew, Frank Matthews. He said Pee Wee was in real estate and owned a number of apartments in New York City. Eventually, we got word that Frank Matthews was a big-time drug dealer in New York City. I suspect Matthews' uncle knew something. Eventually, the uncle divorced Marzella, but he had a good career in our police department."

It appears Matthews' chicken thievery got him in trouble and sent to reform school. According to the story, a white chicken farmer learned that Pee Wee was the ring leader who was costing him money. The man spotted Matthews at the Farmer's Market, got angry and confronted him. Not one to back down, the chicken thief hit the farmer with a brick. Charged with assault, the young boy was hauled into court, but being a juvenile he was sent to reform school and not prison, where he reportedly spent twelve to thirteen months

During his teen years, Matthews picked up a skill that kept him employed until he was able to hit it big in the drug trade. James Bostic, owner of John's Barbershop on Alston Street, said he attended Bull City Barber College in 1961 with Matthews. The barber college was one of three in North Carolina. It was a rigorous preparatory program, according to Bostic, requiring 1500 hours of work and the passing of a state exam to become certified. Students were required to buy their own barber tools. Pee Wee quit the school after a few months. Bostic doesn't know why, but Durham native Robert Bell claims it was because Pee Wee was caught stealing barber equipment. "Not too long after that I saw Matthews on Fayetteville Street," Bell recalled. "He said he was going to New York to make money."

So, while still in his teens, Frank Pee Wee Matthews left his hometown and headed for the glitter of the Big Apple. It would take a few years, however, before the ambitious young man would make his mark on the world.

# TWO

# GO EAST YOUNG MAN

*"I remember Frank as a very muscular and well groomed individual. I was
impressed."*
**Carlos G**

I T IS UNCLEAR when Frank Matthews left Durham in search of his
fortune, but it most likely happened around 1962 or 1963 when the
young man was still in his teens. It is generally believed that Matthews went to Philadelphia first, although some of his homeboys claim
he headed directly for New York City. We will never know for sure the
circumstances of Matthews' departure from his hometown and his arrival
in New York City. After all, there are no records for a crime historian to
peruse, just hearsay and fading memories. One source claimed Matthews
got his mother pregnant. As he explained it, the daughter, his stepsister,
was born in 1963 and Matthews followed the mother to Philadelphia.
This story cannot be substantiated, but it does appear that Matthews
went to Philadelphia first, the most likely scenario has Matthews following his friend Thomas "Cadillac Tommy" Farrington. Like Pee Wee,
Cadillac Tommy was ambitious and charismatic and aspired to be a big-
time gangster.

First arrested for burglary at age 15, Farrington's rap sheet grew over
the next 20 years with offenses ranging from possession of narcotics to
weapons violations, rape and murder. Several of the cases were dismissed,
but on one conviction he was sentenced to serve 20 days to a year for

rape. Interestingly, some Durham sources who knew Matthews and Farrington in their youth say Farrington was in the military and based in Delaware and that Matthews could have gone there first before heading for the City of Brotherly Love. In any case, once settled in Philadelphia, Farrington closely aligned himself with the city's emerging Black Mafia and eventually became an important contact between his buddy Pee Wee and the gang.

Matthews ostensibly spent only about a year in Philadelphia where he reportedly worked as a barber and a runner in the numbers racket. Numbers tickets were often sold out of barber shops. The numbers racket (also known as the policy racket) is an illegal daily lottery in which bets are placed based on the appearance of certain numbers in a statistical listing or tabulation that is published in a daily newspaper or a racing forum. Once the numbers are drawn, the information is given to the bankers who collect the money and pay off winning bets. The lottery is supposed to be illegal, but police corruption and the sheer size of the activity allowed it to flourish.

The numbers racket has had a long history in the black and Hispanic neighborhoods of Philadelphia, as well as in New York City, Chicago, and other cities with large black populations. As early as 1868, Martin Edward Winslow wrote in his *Secrets of the Great City*, "In every district where they live, you will find dingy lottery offices… a negro must play his policy even if his bread is lacking at home."

The lottery has been criticized for taking money from poor people, but in an age of racial discrimination in all sectors of American society, the numbers racket provided Matthews and many other blacks the opportunity for employment. Matthews' low level position in the racket meant that he probably carried the money and betting slips between parlors and the policy headquarters, the so-called numbers or policy bank. Being a runner in the black community allowed Matthews to meet many other young ambitious men who, like himself, were also looking for a profitable hustle. In Philadelphia this included John and Martha Darby, Major Coxson, Tyrone "Fat Ty" Palmer Turk Scott, Foo Foo Ragan, among others, While these contacts would play an important part in his drug empire, it is unclear whether he met them through his own initiative or later through Farrington or some of his other contacts after he moved to New York City.

It appears Matthews had to leave Philly because he got into some kind of trouble with the law. As the story goes, Matthews was arrested by the police and ordered to leave town. How could that happen? The speculation is that Matthews—or some of his associates—had connections and influence within the Philadelphia police department, and they were able to help Matthews get the charges dropped. Whatever the reason, by 1963, or perhaps no later than 1964, Matthews was on his way to New York City. It was a logical move. "New York is a city of opportunity for an ambitious gangster as well as for those who want to make an honest living," explained Roger Garay, a New York City Police Department (NYPD) detective who investigated Frank Matthews. "Frank could cut hair and take numbers bets, but that wouldn't give him the money to realize his boyhood dream of visiting South America."

Arriving in New York City, Matthews settled in Bedford-Stuyvesant and continued to do what he had done in Philly, working as a barber while operating as a numbers runner out of the barbershop where he worked. By now, Frank Matthews was a full grown man: about 5' 8 to 5' 10" tall and 180 pounds in weight and well built. People who knew him recall that his upper body gave him the look of an NFL football running back, although no one ever saw him lift weights. As we know, Matthews had a reputation for toughness and it is believed he moonlighted as an enforcer and a collector of bad debts. Working the streets, the outgoing and charismatic Matthews got to know many of the leading figures of the New York underworld. These contacts eventually helped him move up the criminal ladder.

Matthews' arrival came at a time when America and the Big Apple were experiencing dramatic changes. His criminal career was profoundly affected by these changes, even though he might not have given them much thought. First, America underwent a civil rights revolution that broke down the walls of segregation. Matthews had grown up in Durham when the root of change in race relations took hold. Between 1959 and 1968 America experienced many noted legal and legislative efforts to abolish racial discrimination, beginning with the Brown versus the Board of Education Supreme Court case in 1954 that desegregated the schools and then the Civil Rights Act of 1964. The Voting Rights Act of 1965 further banned racial segregation and unequal application of voter registration requirements, and the Civil Rights Act of 1968 forbade discrimination in the sale and rental of housing.

Still, by the time Matthews arrived in New York City, many blacks had grown disillusioned with the aims of the civil rights movement, and they began espousing black power and black self-determination. This changing, more militant attitude was reflected in all sectors of the African American community, including the gangster element that wanted more control and power over their criminal careers.

Historically until the late 1960s, black criminals in the large urban areas had to settle for a subservient role to their white counterparts. Still, New York City's drug scene did produce some black gangsters who had success in the game in the early 1950s around the time of the Korean War.

Bap Ross even brought some creative and innovative distribution and marketing methods to street level dealing. As Clarence Lusane, the author of *Pipe Dreams Blues: Racism and the War on Drugs*, explained, Ross "established a system whereby pushers to whom he distributed would only be told by one of his workers where to pick up the heroin. The heroin package would be hidden in a hallway or behind a radiator by another of Ross's operatives. Although Ross was eventually caught, these techniques demonstrated the creative ways that dealers could avoid the law and minimize risks." John Freeman, another black dealer, worked with famous Mafia snitch Joseph Valachi until his arrest in 1959.

Today in Harlem, Bumpy Johnson is a legendary figure, a fascinating and complicated gangster who wore several monikers ("Black Outlaw," "Robin Hood of Harlem" and "Black Nationalist"). Lew Rice, a retired DEA agent who was a special agent in charge of the DEA's New York

Division, said, "Johnson was the first original gangster of Harlem and he had a hand in everything, from narcotics to extortion to the gambling rackets. Frank Lucas of *American Gangster* movie fame, who worked for Bumpy Johnson (although the exact nature of that role is in dispute) recalled: "If you wanted to do business in Harlem, you did it with Bumpy or you were dead."

Until the late 1960s, the white Mob ruled Harlem's underworld and Bumpy Johnson had to answer to it. Bumpy essentially was middle man for the Mob and New York's black community. Bumpy's role was to ensure that the Mob would have no problems in the hood. According to Lew Rice, "White Italian gangsters aren't going to feel too comfortable about going to the streets of Harlem to do business. The Mob needed somebody with the respect and resources to handle their business in New York's black community and to collect their money."

But in the mid to late 1960s in New York City, and certainly by the time of Bumpy Johnson's death in 1968, the big-time independent black gangster started to emerge. The first was Leon Aiken who made a fortune in narcotics trafficking in the mid 1960s and shrewdly invested his illicit profits in prime real estate in New York City, Chicago and Los Angeles and a number of legitimate mom and pop businesses in the Big Apple. "My father told me he was a real estate broker," said his son, James Aiken Jr. "He would wake up every morning, put on a suit and leave the house like he was a real businessman."

With the civil rights movement in full swing, Aiken's wealth and charisma made him popular among civic rights activists. His criminal career, however, short-circuited in 1966 when he was charged with drug trafficking and sentenced to 25 years in prison.

James Aiken told his son that the gangster life was the only path open that would allow him to attain and enjoy the good life. "He stuck to the gangster life much longer than he had to," James Aiken Jr. recalled. "I knew he left a million dollars with his sister when he went to prison. My father said that a pocketful of money made him so high he didn't need drugs."

Charles Green was another early independent black gangster who emerged in the mid 1960s. Until his arrest in 1970 on drug trafficking charges, Green operated a group of more than 100 distributors and couriers who trafficked in drugs, mainly in New York state.

As the criminal careers of Aiken and Green show, the opportunities in the drug trade for ambitious black gangsters were opening up big-time, largely because in the turbulent era of the 1950s and 1960s, drug abuse was becoming a big problem in black communities nationwide. About 50 percent of drug addicts in the U.S. were black, the U.S. Narcotics Commission reported in 1959. A decade later, more than a million heroin addicts resided in New York City alone. In the 1960s, Harlem remained an economic trap with no way out for many of its residents, as the heroin plague continued to poison the lives of addicts, their families and the community.

In his book, *Man Child in a Promised Land*, Claude Brown vividly described what was happening to Harlem: "Heroin had just about taken over Harlem. It seemed to be a kind of a plague. Every time I went uptown, somebody else was hooked, somebody else would say…say…'Look here, I got some shit,' meaning heroin. 'Let's get high.' They would say it so casually, the way somebody in another community might say, 'C'mon, let's have a drink.'"

By the mid-1960s, the Vietnam War was in full throttle, and it, too, would have a dramatic impact on the illegal drug trade in the U.S. and exacerbate the growing heroin problem. Clarence Lusane in his study, *Pipe Dreams: Racism and the War on Drugs*, reported that at the height of the famous French Connection, which controlled the heroin distribution into the U.S. from the late 1940s through the 1960s, no more than eight tons of heroin were smuggled into the U.S. each year. But at the height of the Vietnam War in the late 1960s, that figure had risen to 60 tons.

By the early 1970s, nearly 12 percent of the U .S. troops, many of whom were African Americans, were returning stateside as heroin addicts, creating a sizeable market for enterprising African American drug dealers. "Black communities around the country were dealing with a heroin epidemic that threatened to destroy them," Rice explained.

The drug epidemic fueled violence and disorder in the black community. Randy Jurgenson, a retired NYPD officer who served from 1958 to 1977, said the Black Power movement grew in intensity after the killing of Martin Luther King Jr. in 1968. "The year after King's assassination, we had more than 2,000 homicides in New York. The majority of them were in Harlem, and I'd say about 85 percent of them were drug related. It got so bad that if a cop working in Harlem gave someone a summons for double parking, it could easily have led to a small scale riot. That's how close to the edge Harlem was in the late 1960s."

Jurgenson added that the resentment on the street impacted the criminal element. "Drug dealers like Frank Matthews and Nicky Barnes became heroes because people looked upon them as defying a system that didn't work," he explained.

The anger in the black community was fueled by the fact that blacks had few opportunities to make it in the legitimate world. "At this time, America was trying to assure blacks that they could pick themselves up by the bootstraps, but there weren't any bootstraps to do it with," explained Sterling Johnson, an African American federal prosecutor who investigated Frank Matthews before becoming a distinguished federal court judge.

Judge Johnson recalled one experience his father had with the people who controlled the bootstraps. It poignantly sums up the dilemma of the African American at the time. "My father wanted to be a police officer, so he went to a NYPD police station and took the required physical exam. A little while later, the NYPD called my father and said he had a heart murmur and had failed the physical. My father told them, 'I ain't got no heart murmur.' My father was on home relief, which is called welfare these days, but he scratched up enough money to get a doctor to do an independent physical. The test showed he didn't have a heart murmur. My father got a note from the doctor and brought it in person to the police station. They looked at it and said to my father, who was a middle-aged man, 'Boy, if our doctor says you got a heart murmur, you got a heart murmur.'"

In the 1960s, young blacks like Frank Matthews faced the same barriers that the fathers of James Aiken Jr. and Sterling Johnson experienced. Matthews continued to cut hair and take numbers bets to make a living, but he yearned to do something more profitable that would help him realize his big ambitions. Matthews didn't have to look hard to find role models. He saw up close the emerging big time black gangsters and their opulent lifestyles, the money, the beautiful women, the expensive wheels. Like James Aiken, Charles Green and other ambitious brother gangsters in the hood at the time, Frank loved the way money felt in his pockets. "I think Frank woke up one morning and decided to hang up the barber's white jacket," said Garay. "Frank said to himself, 'I'm going to be the dude who wears the $300 silk suits and drives the Lincoln.'"

Matthews was a visionary and could see the fortunes to be had in the booming drug trade, yet Matthews needed the white Mob if he was to get in the drug game. In the mid 1960s, blacks still primarily worked the streets for the white Mob that controlled the supply and distribution of heroin through one of history's biggest monopolies, legit or otherwise, the French Connection.

When Matthews arrived on the New York scene, the illicit drug trade in New York City and the black communities of the East Coast was controlled by big five Italian Mafia families: Gambino, Lucchese, Bonanno, Luciano/Genovese and Profaci/Colombo. But initially, the Jews, not the Italians, dominated big-time crime in America. In the early twentieth century, two of the biggest Jewish mobsters were Arnold Rothstein who became rich as a bootlegger in the 1920s and famous for fixing the 1919 World Series, and Dutch Schultz who took control of the numbers racket in Harlem in the early 1930s and in his brief life (he died at 35) helped extend white Mob influence in Harlem. In the 1920s Jewish gangsters controlled the heroin market, but by the 1930s, La Cosa Nostra had joined the Jewish mobsters in the illegal drug trade. After World War II, La Cosa Nostra took over and began importing its heroin supply from Italian refineries.

When the Italian government banned the manufacture of heroin in Italy in the early 1950s, La Cosa Nostra had to look for other sources.

They developed a new smuggling system whereby morphine base from Turkey was refined in Marseilles and then shipped to New York City or to Montreal, Canada, a city, like the Big Apple, that has a strong La Cosa Nostra presence. So was born the famous French Connection, a powerful narcotics syndicate that was featured into the 1972 Academy Award winning film by the same name, starring Gene Hackman and Roy Schneider. French Corsican gangsters dominated the French Connection through Marseille, one of the busiest ports in the western Mediterranean and a perfect shipping point for contraband and illegal drugs. By the 1940s, as the U.S. sought to mitigate communist influence in France, Marseilles became the post-war heroin capital of the Western World and the linchpin of the French Connection.

One 1960 report showed that while narcotics agents were seizing about 200 pounds of heroin in a typical year, the Corsican traffickers were smuggling in that amount every other week. The French Connection was, in effect, the only real sizeable organized smuggling ring, and it allowed the Italian Mob to monopolize the heroin trade from the 1960s through the early 1970s. The Corsicans then would supply Frank Matthews with heroin, helping to make him the biggest drug kingpin in the U.S. How he did that became one of the remarkable chapters in organized crime history.

Initially, Matthews tried the traditional route to breaking into the game. As writer Donald Goddard explained in *Easy Money*, "With a piece of a policy bank, he could reasonably expect to earn about $100,000 annually, but there were 18-year old punks making much more by simply turning a load of narcotics. But this young ambitious would-be drug lord knew that to get the money to break into the trade he would have to get it from the dominant money source at the time: La Cosa Nostra."

To do that, Matthews had to show the white Mob that he had the resources and ability to put together a deal that met its strict terms: 30 percent down on a drug deal with the balance paid in cash upon delivery of the heroin. Such a deal involved a lot of risk for Matthews. Indeed, death would be the consequence if he screwed up and did not pay back the money to the Mob.

Remarkably, Matthews managed to get an audience with members of two of the crime families: the Gambinos and Bonnanos. The godfathers listened to Matthews' pitch, but for whatever reason, turned him down. Normally, this should have been the end of the line for the young ambitious gangster, but Matthews' charisma, hustle and networking paid off.

Spanish Raymond Marquez, the biggest numbers king in New York City, took a liking to Matthews and helped open doors for him. Marquez had operated in the numbers since 1947, the year he graduated from high school. Although Spanish Raymond has consistently denied it, his rise in the numbers benefited from his relationship with La Cosa Nostra mobster Fat Tony Salerno, who once ran the numbers in East Harlem and eventually rose in the early 1980s to become the head of the Genovese crime family. In 1970, the *New York Times* reported that Marquez was paying five percent of his profits to Salerno because anybody who operated in New York numbers had to pay Fat Tony something.

Spanish Raymond's first arrest came in July 1957 when he was jailed briefly for refusing to testify before a grand jury about police corruption. The runners were usually paid a straight salary of about $100 to $200 a week. One of Spanish Raymond's banks raided by the police had betting value that sometimes reached $100,000 a day. Police officials estimated the total value of his operation to be about $25 million annually and put the profit margin of a numbers network at about 15 percent. Thus, in 1970 the Marquez operation was netting about $3.7 million annually.

Between 1958 and 1967, Marquez was arrested on charges of operating a numbers shop, assault, bribery, and consorting with known criminals, although he was not convicted on any of them. He operated freely until the FBI began investigating him in earnest in the mid-1960s as part of a national crackdown on organized crime. On July 10, 1967, he was jailed for refusing to answer questions posed by a New York grand jury investigating ties between gamblers and police. Marquez even refused to answer when the grand jury gave him immunity from prosecution.

"Spanish Raymond operated out of the 28th Precinct, and he was a legend in New York City," explained Jurgenson. "New York's black community looked upon the numbers king as a friend of the community."

By the late 1960s, police reports indicated that Spanish Raymond's numbers operation was thriving; in fact, New York law enforcement listed his operation as New York City's fifth largest. Centered around Eighth Avenue and 113th Street in Harlem, the operation included five numbers banks or offices, at least 400 runners to collect bets from customers, and 27 controllers who collected the bets from the runners. The controllers kept about 35 percent of the bets for themselves before sending the information about the bets to the main office bank via a pickup man.

It is believed Spanish Raymond put Matthews in touch with his Cuban friend Rolando Gonzalez, at the time one of the biggest drug traffickers in New York City. Carlos G., who doesn't want his real name used because he is an illegal immigrant, knew Rolando Gonzalez well. Gonzalez and Carlos and his family had all fled Cuba in the early 1960s after Fidel Castro took power. Carlos G. met Gonzalez for the first time in 1968 at his cousin's house. They hit it off, although Carlos was a teenager and Gonzalez was several years older. Carlos was impressed with Gonzalez the first time he met him. "Rolando was handsome, stocky and swarthy looking," Carlos recalled. He was in his 50s but he had an attractive 18-year old wife named Esmeralda. He wore a lot of jewelry and expensive clothes and drove a Cadillac. He was very charismatic and self-assured, but he was still a gentleman. I later learned that Rolando had been a pimp in Cuba. At the time I met him he was the man for cocaine in New York City."

Because of Carlos' age, Rolando did not want Carlos to peddle drugs for him. He did allow Carlos, though, to make one delivery to Frank Matthews at the Taft Hotel. Matthews paid Carlos about $3,000 for the delivery. "I remember Frank as a very muscular and well groomed individual," Carlos recalled. "I was impressed."

Carlos saw Matthews a second time when Gonzales came by his cousin's house again to help Carlos celebrate his 18th birthday. Gonzalez brought an ounce of cocaine and a half gallon of Chevas Regal scotch with him and put it on the table. Matthews dropped by a little later to see Rolando about some business matter. Carlos watched Rolando and Mathews drink some scotch and engage in an intense conversation. When they finished they began laughing and joking around. "You could see they liked each other," Carlos recalled. "Frank snorted some cocaine right in front of me."

The law was closing in on Gonzalez and in 1969 he was indicted for drug trafficking. Not too long after, Gonzalez packed two suitcases and jumped bail, fleeing to Venezuela where he had plenty of contacts in the drug trade. "I knew that not long after Rolando paid two FBI agents $20,000 apiece to give him 24 hours to get out of the country," Carlos recalled, "Carlos packed his bags and fled for Venezuela. I never ran into Frank Matthews again."

Arriving in Caracas, Venezuela, Gonzalez settled into his comfortable apartment on the Avenida Andres Bello and had no problem resuming his life as a big-time drug dealer. Venezuela was one of two countries in Latin America (the other was Brazil) that had established branches of Italy's La Cosa Nostra. Given that pedigree and its strategic location, Venezuela was the ideal base for moving French Connection heroin to Latin America.

This job was mainly done through the Union Corse, a tight knit criminal organization that originated in the hills of Corsica and eventually became centered in Marseilles. A September 1972 *Time* magazine expose described the Union Corse as dominating the worldwide trafficking in narcotics, particularly the supply and processing of heroin flowing into the U.S. from France, South America and Southeast Asia. Though weak in the U.S. during the Matthews era, the Union Corse was more powerful than La Cosa Nostra in many parts of the world. The Corsicans' big strength was their ability to infiltrate and corrupt governments at all levels, from ministers to judges to customs officials. This influence allowed the Union Corse to protect the heroin that it moved from Marseille.

Many Corsicans were strongly anti-fascist during World War 11, but several of them, most notably August Ricord, a French Connection founding member, collaborated with the Nazis. After the war, the CIA recruited many of them to help the U.S. battle its new enemy: Soviet communism. After Fidel Castro took power in Cuba in 1959, the U.S was outraged when he set up a communist state. Venezuela became an important listening post for the CIA as Uncle Sam monitored Cuban activities and sought to overthrow the Castro regime. Beginning about 1962, several of the Corsican Nazi collaborators began migrating to Venezuela, Brazil, Panama and other Latin American countries. Ironically, the CIA had helped to forge the French Connection in which the Corsicans played such an important role.

It was these same Corsicans with whom Matthews would collaborate, making him an important broker between the Corsicans who manufactured the heroin and the Cubans who were making Miami the major port of entry for French Connection heroin and cocaine from South America.

In early July 1972 Matthews made a visit to Caracas, and Miguel Garcia, one of the key traffickers in Miami and an associate of the Corsican in Venezuela, booked him into the Hotel Club Americana. Matthews was impressed with the way the Corsicans had set up the narcotics pipeline. Matthews did not know it, but the Corsican—CIA-French Connection triangle would eventually make him part of the Cold War tug of war.

After taking care of business, Matthews spent the rest of his time in Caracas, relaxing with a harem of women and an ample supply of cocaine before his hosts put him back on a plane to the U.S. Agents from the U.S. Bureau of Narcotics and Dangerous Drugs (BNDD) who were stationed in Caracas took note of Matthews' visit. Matthews was now under investigation by the U.S. government and his phones were wiretapped. Back in the U.S., he was recorded talking to Sheila Frazier, the actress who starred in the famous Superfly movie of the early 1970s. Strangely, Matthews had booked his flight under Frankie McNeal, his mother's maiden name, and he used the same name when he filled out his customs declaration. Yet he traveled with a passport in his own name: Frank Larry Mathews. Apparently, no customs official had noted the difference.

# THREE

# BECOMING A KINGPIN

*"Frank Matthews is a legend. His story is remarkable."*
**Ike Atkinson, former drug kingpin**

THROUGH HIS VENEZUELAN connections, Rolando Gonzalez undoubtedly helped Frank Matthews become a kingpin, but it is unclear how Matthews officially entered the game. According to reports, Gonzalez became Matthews' principal supplier, helping him move loads of heroin and cocaine from Latin America. Still, we have no way to confirm this, given the time that has elapsed and the lack of informative sources from the Matthews era.

As authorities persued their investigation of Matthews, his sources of drug supply largely remained a mystery. They did have leads to possible contacts who could have helped Matthews with distribution, money laundering, production supplies or other "services," but when they investigated, the trail went cold. "We knew that Frank Matthews was working with some gangsters in Brooklyn," revealed William Callahan, a special attorney with ODALE (Office of Drug Abuse Law Enforcement), a division of the U.S. Department of Justice. "What was the nature of that association? We never did find out." Roger Garay, a member of the task force that investigated Matthews, said Matthews had a contact, an Italian businessman, to whom Matthews referred in phone conversations as "Mr. IBM." We had Frank on the wire, but he was always very careful when he referred to Mr. IBM. We never learned his identity," Garay said.

The heroin pipeline in the Matthews era was often volatile, and its delivery, unpredictable. In the late 1960s, the French Connection, the main source of heroin after World War II, was beginning to lose its stranglehold on the heroin trade, for the authorities in the U.S. and abroad were having great success in disrupting it. Opium, the raw material for heroin manufacturing, came from Turkey, and in 1968 the country agreed to limit the opium production. Three days later, Turkey agreed to a complete ban. Meanwhile, law enforcement in France and the U.S. managed to pull off a number of high profile busts. By 1972, authorities had busted several illicit heroin labs in France and seized millions of dollars, and the once smooth operating French Connection was in shambles. The results were soon evident in a heroin shortage on the U.S. East Coast.

The drug supply was sometimes so uncertain that Matthews' organization would buy heroin from some unlikely sources. For Matthews, this included Ike Atkinson's organization, according to DEA reports. Ike Atkinson, a kingpin in his own right, operated out of Bangkok in the time of the Matthews era and sold China white heroin, at the time the purest heroin on the planet. The DEA estimated that Atkinson's organization smuggled nearly $400 million worth of heroin from Southeast Asia to the U.S. between 1968 and 1975.

Atkinson, who had the moniker "Sergeant Smack," was connected to the infamous heroin-cadaver conspiracy popularized in the movie *American Gangster,* the largely fictional story of gangster Frank Lucas. As this author showed in his book, *Sergeant Smack,* the heroin-cadaver conspiracy was a hoax; in fact, the smuggling of drugs via coffins and the bodies of dead American soldiers from the Vietnam War never happened. Strangely, Frank Matthews was rumored to be connected to that conspiracy. "When we learned Matthews had contacts in the military, we checked out to see if there was a connection to any heroin-cadaver conspiracy, but we found nothing," Callahan said.

Much has been made of Matthews being the first black drug dealer to work independently of La Cosa Nostra. This is not exactly true. It was actually Atkinson who worked completely independently of the white Mob. Ike Atkinson never did meet Matthews, but he learned a lot about Black Caesar in prison. "He is a legend," Atkinson recalled. "His story is remarkable."

Two aspects of Matthews' brilliance as a gangster were his shrewdness and practicality, and he exhibited these qualities in his relationship with the Mob. Seth Ferranti, true crime writer and creator of the *Gorilla Convict* blog and web site who has written extensively about black gangsters, said: "Matthews was nobody's gofer, and he was not content to be the pawn of the Mafia like so many other black men before him. But Matthews recognized that dealing with the Mafia was to his benefit. So he used them when he needed to. The Mafia considered Frank 'an uppity nigger' but he had the clout and the organization to do as he pleased, and the Mob couldn't risk warfare with him."

Although Matthews was known for his dislike of the La Cosa Nostra, he developed good relations with at least one white Italian-American mobster: Louis Cirillo. It is believed that Matthews might have been introduced to the Mob by Cirillo. As the story goes, Matthews went to the white Mob and tried to show them that he had the resources and what it took to deal with on credit terms: 30 percent down on any drug deal and the balance paid in cash on the delivery of the heroin. Such a deal involved a lot of risk for Matthews; death would be the consequence if he could not pay the money back.

But there is no way of knowing for sure whether this actually happened. As of this writing, the 88-year old Cirillo is retired and living in Florida, and he has never talked about or written anything about his days as a big-time gangster drug dealer. Word is that Cirillo is planning a book and expecting big money if he is to reveal the secrets of the crime scene during the Matthews era.

Today, many old-time black drug dealers from the late 1960s-early 1970s era remain in contact with Cirillo. They say the former mobster is still a standup guy. "When I was in prison, some brothers told me about Louis," explained Atkinson, who spent 32 years in prison on drug trafficking charges. "They told me he always had the stuff when you couldn't find it. You'd always see Louie in the yard talking to some black guy." Atkinson spent time with Cirillo at Atlanta Federal Penitentiary.

Cirillo was known to be an excellent source for a drug deal. In their book, *The Marseilles Mafia: The Truth Behind the World of Drug Trafficking*, Pierre Galante and Louis Sapin wrote of Cirillo: "He was the ideal buyer. Never the slightest delay in payment, never the slightest quibble, except sometimes (on Cirillo's part) in connection with the quality of the goods delivered. But then he would prove that his customers were justified. Whatever the size of the deal, he seemed to have an inexhaustible stack of hundred dollar bills available. He had been known to pay out at least 3 million dollars in a single day, in ready cash, for a single delivery."

Born in 1924 New York City, Louis Cirillo was an old school mobster, low key and tight lipped. He lived in the Bronx and claimed he was a simple baker who operated a bagel bakery in Manhattan and earned a couple of thousand dollars a week, good money in the Matthews era but nowhere close to the millions authorities say he earned from his criminal activities. "You don't hear much about Louie Cirillo today, but he was about as big a player as they had back then," said a friend of Cirillo who keeps in close touch with him.

In the late 1960s, when Matthews began to make his mark in the drug game, Cirillo had a special relationship within La Cosa Nostra. Four of the five principal Mob families—the Bonannos, Tramuntis, Genoveses and Colombos—gave Cirillo a monopoly over the heroin supplyed to their respective drug rings. At the time it was estimated to be about one-sixth of U.S. consumption. Cirillo and his associates smuggled drugs in from Italy, France and Latin America, raking in hundreds of millions of dollars. While Cirillo may not have started Matthews in the drug game, he was reported to have sold Matthews his last kilo of heroin before Matthews jumped bail and disappeared.

However Matthews broke into the drug game—Rolando Gonzalez, Louie Cirillo or some other source—once he did, his rise was meteoric. "He was a country boy at heart, but I don't think New York City or the drug game was ready for a ballsy, astute guy like him," Ferranti said. "His simple beginnings shaped and prepped him and inspired him to become the man he became. To him the big city must have seemed like a jungle when he arrived, but it was a jungle where he would become king. "

Within a year, he was on his way to being New York City's biggest dealer. He exhibited brilliant organizational skills and a shrewd ability to forge productive relationships with other gangsters. He looked upon himself as a businessman, not an ordinary drug dealer. "His personality and charisma got him connections around the country," explained Alan Bradley (aka Al Profit) , co-director of the award-winning documentary, *The Frank Matthews Story*. "People liked Frank and they liked money. Given that he was a natural born leader, they were willing to follow his lead." Clinton "Shorty" Buise, a gambler from Baltimore during the Matthews era who knew Black Caesar, explained, "Frank had good social skills and he did a lot of favors for people. He made it possible for a lot of people to make a living and have a lot of things."

Black Caesar had a reputation for toughness, but, despite some vicious battles for turf in the early 1970s, he seemed to use his brain and vision rather than violence to get ahead in the drug game. "Some sources told us that Frank committed murders, but we could never tie one to him," Garay said. Bradley added: "Matthews was a manipulator, not a killer. A master strategist and tactician with a great sense of the big picture of what he was trying to do. You heard rumors of violence around him, but none of those stories have real credibility."

Callahan said Matthews didn't have to pull the trigger. "Violence didn't bother him, but he didn't have to kill," Callahan explained. "He had several associates who would kill for him in a heart beat. All he had to do was say the word."

Still, the gangster element was wary about disappointing or double-crossing Black Caesar. "We would arrest street dealers in Bed-Sty and it was amazing to see how fearful they were of Frank and his lieutenants," Garay recalled.

The gangster scene in New York City in Matthews' era was much different than what we have today. "It wasn't as cut throat, "said Rick Talley, a former drug dealer who knew Matthews. "We hung around together, we partied together, we drank in the same bars together. Nothing like the crazy stuff and turf wars we saw beginning in the crack era of the '80s."

Liddy Jones, a former Baltimore drug kingpin who bought dope from Matthews, knew several of Black Caesar's' associates. He recalls how different the era was compared to what followed. "We were competitors but we got along," Jones said. "It wasn't dog-eat-dog like the crack era eventually became. We weren't trying to kill each other. We hung out together, even partied together."

Matthews would buy drugs from any source, provided the product was of good quality. He was not a greedy man and did not operate like La Cosa Nostra, which sold drugs at inflated prices and did not care about the product's quality. As Donald Goddard explained, "Matthews was always willing to pay premium prices for multi-kilo shipments of pure heroin, all the way down to bundles of three percent street bags, if that was the best he could find."

Matthews' attractive common-law wife, Barbara Hinton, had an accounting background, and took care of the organization's finances. As Matthews moved about wheeling and dealing, anyone wanting drugs from the Matthews organization had to deal with Barbara Hinton. She would connect them with one of Matthews' lieutenants for their heroin supply. "Barbara knew how to do the books and keep track of the money," said Roger Garay.

Matthews' associates from that era speak warmly of Barbara Hinton. "I knew Barbara Hinton personally," recalled Big Head Brother Carter, one of Frank Matthews' biggest customers. "She was a lovely lady. I believe she was from Florida. We later went to trial together."

"Matthews was a homeboy in the truest sense. He was more comfortable working with people who came from his hometown, especially if he knew them. Given his country roots, he trusted his own kind," Garay explained. "He sought out homeboys, those guys he knew from the Durham area and those who became friends as he worked his way to the top.

He would accept working with strangers if they came with a recommendation from someone he knew well."

Several homeboys from Durham would trek to the Big Apple to look up Pee Wee and get a job or score some dope to sell on their own. They included Charles Swayzy Cameron, who became one of Matthews most trusted associates and distributors in North Carolina: Pedro Currington, who at one time played professional football; Pete Thorp who worked in the Ponderosa, one of Matthews' heroin processing mills; William Fred Cameron (aka Babe), a former moonshiner who started out by buying heroin from Thorp; and Gattis Hinton, who at one time ran the Ponderosa cutting mill and who would later disappear at the time Mathews jumped bond. One BNDD report described James Olive Rowland (aka John Lilly) as the "biggest heroin and cocaine dealer in North Carolina." It further described Rowland as an investor in a vending machine operation owned by Matthews, a buyer of his drugs.

Matthews controlled the cutting, packaging and sale of heroin in every major East Coast city. Much of Matthews' product was processed and packaged at two main drug mills, both located in Brooklyn: one at 925 Prospect Place (nicknamed the "Ponderosa") and the another at 106 East 56th Street (nicknamed the "OK Corral"). Each day as many as forty workers were bused to the mills, where, for about $100 a day, they bagged heroin and cocaine while using masks to protect them from sniffing the cocaine they packaged. The mill was built like Fort Knox, its walls reinforced with steel and concrete and protected by submachine guns and two elephant guns. According to federal court records, "The Matthews' organization cut the heroin and cocaine to the addict level and packaged it and then sold it to street-level distribution organizations in the metropolitan area and beyond, thereby eliminating the middleman and increasing the profit of the organization."

By the early 1970s, Matthews' organization was handling multi-ton shipments in at least 21 states, according to the U.S. government reports. Matthews' empire extended along the east coast (Boston, New York City, Philadelphia, Connecticut and Baltimore) to the midwest (Chicago and

Cincinnati) to the Carolinas, Georgia and Alabama in the south and as far west as St. Louis. "Matthews' drug pipeline never reached California, but in time Matthews would have ruled the U.S.," Callahan said.

The profits that drug dealers made from Matthews' heroin and cocaine were staggering. In 1971 one drug gang alone was buying as much as five kilos of heroin at a time from Matthews at prices up to $26,000 a kilo. The gang would then sell about 17,500 bags to as many as 10,000 retail customers at a gross of about $45,000. No gangster in New York City during the Matthews era made more money. "The Italian Mafia made a lot of money but they couldn't touch Frank," Liddy Jones said. "He had more money than the Mob."

Some dealers were paying Matthews about $250,000 in cash for a single deal. Callahan said, "If Matthews' wings hadn't been clipped as they were in 1972, he would have eventually dominated the national scene and then he would have become a truly international kingpin. I think Matthews was so ambitious that could have been his ultimate goals."

Matthews operated like a McDonald's or a Domino's Pizza, setting up franchises in the cities of its expanding network and hiring qualified locals to manage them. William Beckwith from Brooklyn was the major lieutenant who worked closely with Matthews and oversaw the OK Corral processing mill in Brooklyn. His main man in New Haven, Connecticut was Scarvey McCargo, who at times would come to the Ponderosa drug mill and help out. Nate Elder was Matthews' key associate in Georgia, and Frank would go often to Atlanta for pleasure, to keep an eye on real estate interests, and to meet Elder on business. Donald Conner managed his business in Queens, New York.

Since the Big Apple was the biggest and most important market for narcotics, Matthews worked with several big-time drug dealers. Dickie Diamond knew Frank since 1969 and beginning in early 1970 did business with Matthews mainly through Beckwith. Ray Daniels (aka Dutch Schultz) received between 100 and 150 kilos of heroin from the Matthews organization via Donald Keno James, his chief lieutenant.

James Carter, another upper-level associate, acted as the major distributor in Maryland, overseeing a sub-cadre of connections in that state, while David Bates was Matthews' man in Pennsylvania. Shelby Cotton (aka Jimmy Terry) and James Perry Craven were Matthews' two biggest customers in Chicago and Cincinnati respectively. Zach Robinson, a former boxer, supplied much of Pittsburg with Matthews' dope. "Zach was a tough guy, a former boxer with 27 heavyweight fights," said Jimmy Harris, a retired DEA agent who investigated Robinson. "He was one of the biggest dealers in the eastern U.S."

Outside of New York City, Baltimore and Philadelphia were Matthews' two biggest markets, and in each city he worked with several key associates eager to get rich or die trying. In Baltimore, Liddy Jones and Big Head Brother Carter, two of the biggest Baltimore drug kingpins in the Matthews era, became two of Matthews most important customers in the city.

In the early 1970s, drug dealer Liddy Jones had sources for his heroin supply, but he could not get enough of it to meet the demand. "I had a good friend who said she knew somebody in Brooklyn who could get me all the smack I needed," Jones recalled. "My friend was tight with Mickey Beckwith, Frank's man, I asked for five keys and I got it for $22,000 a key. I began making real good money from my connection to Frank Matthews. I learned I wasn't anything special. All the top drug dealers along the east coast were getting their dope from Frank."

Big Head Brother Carter was perhaps Matthews' biggest customer in Baltimore. "I met Frank through a guy named Reggie Davis," Carter recalled. "One day, Reggie brought Frank Matthews by my place. Frank offered a better price for his drugs than anybody I was dealing with at the time...$19,000 a kilo."

Maryland legislator James Turk Scott, a bail bondsman, a political and courthouse insider who knew all the big players in Baltimore, was another associate to whom Matthews sold dope. Scott was shot to death on July 13, 1973, inside a garage at his hi-rise apartment, located in the swank Bolton Hill area of Baltimore. Flyers, 8 by 11 inches in size, were strewn over the body. The text of the flyer read: "Selling drugs is an act of treason. The penalty for treason is death."

A shadowy group calling itself "Black October" claimed responsibility. At the time Turk was facing a federal indictment on charges of conspiracy to transport 40 pounds of heroin from New York City to Baltimore. Matthews case investigators suspected that Matthews might have had something to do with Scott's death because of a drug deal gone bad, but Sherman Dobson, a 20-year old Howard University student and son of a prominent Maryland minster was charged.

In Philadelphia, Major Benjamin Coxson, a hustler, entrepreneur, drug financier, mover and shaker, and some would say fraudster, was one of the most colorful Matthews' associates. Another key associate, Tyrone Fat Palmer, became known as "Mr. Millionaire" for the way he made money from the high grade Matthews dope he sold to Philadelphia's Black Mafia.

John "Pop" Darby played an important role in finding the cutting agents Matthews needed for processing his heroin. Tom Farrington was a homeboy who established a connection with Philadelphia's powerful Black Mafia. Major Bejamin Coxson was a well-connected local who had a promising political career but opted instead for the path of criminality, with unfortunate consequences. Foo Foo Ragan's career as a gangster would have a shocking conclusion.

Pop worked closely with Walter Rosenbaum, who supplied the Matthews organization with mannite and quinine, the cutting agents used in heroin processing. On several occasions, Rosenbaum handled the entire Darby family's bail bond needs when they got in trouble with the law. "Rosenbaum's partner was Perry Royster, the so-called 'Big Man,'" Garay explained. "He owned an exterminating company that he used as a cover to smuggle in pounds and pounds of quinine and lactose, necessary ingredients for both heroin and cocaine manufacturing." After agreeing to help Darby, Rosenbaum contacted a company called Schneiner Drugs and the Italian trade commission in New York City so he could obtain the names of companies in Italy that produced mannite.

On June 26, 1972, a shipment of mannite arrived in Philadelphia from Italy. Four days later, on instructions from Rosenbaum, Darby had the mannite delivered to a grocery store in Newark, New Jersey. Pleased with the deal, Darby asked Rosenbaum to get him more mannite. Rosenbaum also contacted various organizations in the New York City area to obtain quinine for the Matthews organization, but without success.

In 1972, Darby asked Rosenbaum to form the Herald Corporation for the purpose of buying stock in a bank that was about to be formed in Philadelphia. Matthews wanted to invest in the bank so his organization could use it to launder its narcotics profits. Matthews and Darby each invested $15,000 in the venture.

Matthews may have avoided violence, but the same could not be said for several of his associates. It is remarkable how many of them went down. Born in South Carolina in 1948, Matthews associate Fat Ty Palmer began dealing drugs in 1966. Police arrested him three times and on July 7, 1971, he was sentenced to prison for two to seven years but was released pending appeal. By then, he had become a successful independent trafficker and big player on the Philadelphia criminal scene, thanks largely to the Matthews connection. He also led a high profile lifestyle that included parties, attractive women and fancy late-model Cadillacs.

A gangster named James P.I. Smith sold Palmer about $240,000 worth of cocaine that he had taken on consignment from Palmer, but a Smith associate named Harris stiffed him, and so Smith could not pay Palmer. In February 1972, gunmen found Harris drinking in a North Philadelphia bar and shot him dead. Philadelphia police received information that Smith was responsible.

Palmer was still out $240,000, and rumors spread that Palmer had put a $15,000 contract on Smith's life. On March 2, police found Smith in a parking lot with two bullet holes in his head. Believing he had taken care of business, Fat Ty thought he had nothing to worry about. About a month later, he went out for a good time at Atlantic City's Club Harlem, a popular venue that hosted some of the country's greatest rhythm and blues acts and attracted Philadelphia's mainstream and gangster elite. That night, Billy Paul headlined the bill, and the Club was packed with 600 to 800 patrons, including Tyrone Palmer, his bodyguard and an entourage of young women. A group of five men sat across the room looking menacingly at Palmer's table. Then the five men got up, and led by Sam Christian, their leader, walked across the floor.

Sam Christian, a thick necked, 215 pound bull of a man and former Black Panther, founded the Philadelphia Black Mafia in September 1968. From its humble beginnings holding up grocery stores and card games, the Black Mafia moved into extortion, prostitution and eventually into the booming drug trade. Brutal and violent, the Black Mafia carried out numerous murders, including those of seven Hanafi Muslims at the home of NBA basketball great Kareem Abdul Jabbar on January 18, 1973.

When Christian and his men reached Palmer's table, an argument ensued. Christian reportedly shot Palmer in the face as he tried to rise out of his chair. Palmer's bodyguard Gilbert Malik Satterwhite reached for his gun but was shot dead. More gunfire was exchanged. Mayhem ensued as the crowd scurried and scrambled for cover or the exit. Christian and his Black Mafia coharts fled the nightclub. Once outside, they exchanged gunfire with the police. Five people (Palmer and Satterwhite and three girlfriends) died, and more than 20 people were wounded. A warrant was issued for Christian's arrest, but he had fled the city. Victims and potential witnesses refused to come forward, and no one was ever arrested for the murders.

The Club Harlem incident was never fully explained, but it showed the growing power of Philly's Black Mafia. Matthews was supposed to be in Atlantic City at the Club Harlem that night, but fortunately for him, he never made it.

Born in 1928, Major Benjamin Coxson had moved with his family to Philadelphia in 1942. When barely out of his teens, Coxson showed his amazing entrepreneurial skills by successfully owning and operating car washes, car lots and several other automobile related endeavors. Coxson boasted, "People credit me with being a good super salesman. They say I have the ability to sell ice to Eskimos, fire to the devil, sand to the Arab."

Among the people Coxson counted as his friends and associates were Angelo Bruno, La Cosa Nostra chief of Philadelphia and South Jersey, and boxing great Muhammad Ali. But Coxson's shady activities and his willingness to hustle on both sides of the law landed him in jail for a variety of fraud-related offenses. In all, Coxson was convicted ten times and spent nearly two years in the federal penitentiary at Lewisburg, Pennsylvania. Remarkably, Coxson still managed to run for mayor of Camden, New Jersey. When asked about his criminal record, he replied with a laugh, "Most politicians start out as office holders and wind up getting arrested. I aim to reverse that process." Coxson finished a distant seventh out of a field of nine candidates.

On May 29, 1973, two young men were found executed at a hotel in North Philadelphia. Police believe Coxson had ordered the hits himself after a drug deal had gone bad. By then Coxson owned a lavish house in Camden, New Jersey, in the Cherry Hill section at 1146 Barbara Drive. He lived there with his girlfriend, Lois Robinson Luby, and her three children by an ex-husband. On June 28, 1973, intruders entered the home and tied Coxson up. They then shot him once in the back of the head while he was kneeling beside his waterbed. Luby, her 15-year old daughter Lita and 14-year old son Toro were also shot. Lois and Toro survived but Lita died a week later at Cherry Hill Medical Center.

The youngest of Lois' children, 13-year old Lex, was also bound hand and foot, but he managed to hop away from the Coxson house and alert a neighbor, who called the police. Lex told the police that four black men in the black Cadillac came by the house at 4 a.m., honking their car horn. Coxson woke up and let them in. Then the murdering began.

About three weeks after the massacre, police arrested Ronald Harvey, a member of the Black Mafia who was already under suspicion for the killing of the seven Hanafi Muslims in Washington, DC. Harvey was identified as one of the four men in the Black Cadillac that June morning at Coxson's house.

"The Black Mafia had Coxson killed because he pissed them off," explained one source. "Coxson failed to work out a deal between the Mafia in New York and the local Muslims. He cost them a lot of money." Harvey became a fugitive before he was finally caught and brought to trial in November 1974. He was convicted and sentenced to life in prison.

The murder of his homeboy Tommy Farrington must have hurt Matthews the most. Like Palmer and Coxson, Farrington seemed to have run afoul of the powerful Black Mafia by not paying protection money. The Black Mafia had talked to Farrington about the "oversight," and he agreed to meet them at the Club Paree to deal with the problem. As Farrington talked with friends outside the bar, a man sneaked up behind him, started shooting and kept shooting as Farrington lay on the ground. Farrington was hit by four bullets. The killer fled. Farrington was rushed to Temple Hospital where he was pronounced dead.

No one was ever charged and the case remained unsolved, but police received information from informants who fingered "Black Charlie" Russell as the mastermind in Farrington's murder, which was committed by George Bo Abney.

So dangerous had the situation become in Philadelphia that Matthews thought it best to move John Darby from Philly to Brooklyn for his own safety. Black Caesar would not retaliate. The Black Mafia had become too powerful. As in other urban areas with black populations, Philadelphia's most powerful gang was taking back the hood from outside gangster elements.

# FOUR

# A LIVING LEGEND IS MADE

*"If he had had the opportunity and had gone the legitimate route, he could have bought one McDonald's franchise and that Macdonald's would have become five, ten... thirty Mcdonald's... I have no doubt about that."*
**Roger Garay, Group 12 investigator**

F IVE YEARS AFTER arriving in New York City, Frank Matthews was on his way to reigning as the Big Apple's biggest drug kingpin. He was still in his early 20s, but he exhibited entrepreneurial skills well beyond his years. He had established his own drug connection in Venezuela, an accomplishment that for a young African American in the late 1960s seemed impossible to achieve, given the still powerful reach of La Cosa Nostra. A drug connection gave Matthews tremendous leverage in the underworld. As Shorty Buise, a former Baltimore gambler who knew Frank Matthews, explained, "In the world of crime, a drug connection is sacred. You really had something."

Matthews' criminal career was so meteoric that in the early 1970s, he acquired the moniker of Black Caesar, a name given to him, it is said, as recognition of his resemblance to the persona of Julius Caesar, the great Roman Emperor. Like Caesar, Matthews impressed people with his style, charisma and determination. In the 1971 blaxploitation movie, *Black Caesar*, Matthews was allegedly said to be the role model for the character Tommy Gibbs played by Fred Williamson. Gibbs is a tough kid, who, unlike Matthews, grows up in the urban ghetto but, like Matthews, aspires to be a kingpin gangster. While they are both unwilling to accept the lowly racist role American society has assigned to them, Gibbs, but not Matthews, becomes a part of the Italian Mafia. As the movie progresses, Gibbs establishes a criminal empire, challenges the Mob and eventually sets off a gang war. If Matthews had hung out a little longer on the New York scene, his criminal career might have ended like that of Tommy Gibbs. Instead, in his relatively brief appearance, Black Caesar managed to carve out a criminal career that has made him a living legend.

Seth Ferranti, author of the *Street Legends* book series and the creator of the *Gorilla Convict* blog and website, has researched the Frank Matthews story, and he believes that with the rise of Martin Luther King and the civil rights movement and later the Black Panthers, the timing was right for the advent of the black drug kingpin in the late 1960s. "Black people were feeling proud and had a lot of nationalist movement going where blacks were stepping up in society and taking charge of their own destiny," he explained. "The '60s era was radical in many ways, and it did a lot for the black gangster as well as the black law-abiding citizen. The black gangster wanted to step out from under the thumb of the Italian Mob, be the boss and make money."

The incredible amounts of money Matthews made from the drug game allowed him to do things, live a lavish lifestyle and grow into the Black Caesar persona, while becoming a living legend. In the beginning, however, after arriving in New York City, his manner was low-key and his lifestyle relatively modest. As Black Caesar began his ascent in the drug trade, he moved into a modest three bedroom apartment at 130 Clarkson Avenue in the Flatbush section of Brooklyn. The apartment building was populated by mostly white working-class people of modest income. "In those days, Matthews did not really stick out in a crowd," recalled Rick Talley, a former New York City drug dealer who first met Matthews in the late 1960s. "In the way he was dressed, the way he talked, Frank looked and moved more like a country kid from North Carolina than a polished gangster."

Buise said Matthews seemed to skyrocket to notoriety out of nowhere. "You never heard of Matthews until about 1968 or 1969 and then his name began "ringing like a doorbell in the hood," Buise explained.

By this time, Matthews was expanding his criminal business empire from his base in the Big Apple to other cities and states, building strategic alliances and hauling in the profits that made him truly America's first black godfather. "Matthews was an entrepreneur by any measure of the term," explained Roger Garay, a NYPD detective who investigated Matthews. "If he had had the opportunity and had gone the legitimate route, he could have bought one McDonald's franchise and that McDonald's would have become five, ten… thirty McDonald's…I have no doubt of that."

Seth Ferranti believes that Black Caesar had all the attributes that could have made him a Steve Jobs or Bill Gates of the legitimate business world: diplomatic skills, mental toughness, flexibility and adaptability. Ferranti, a former gangster himself and now incarcerated in federal prison, elaborated, "Frank lived by two maxims important in the drug game. His word was always good and he had balls. You can rise in the drug game if you have both those attributes."

It is the measure of the man, that everybody, associate and competitor alike, respected and liked Frank Matthews. "In dealing with Frank, you always knew that his word was good," said Liddy Jones. "It was amazing to make a deal with him. He never really counted the money. You could have shorted him thousands of dollars and Frank wouldn't have known. I don't think he would have cared. But it's that kind of style that makes you want to trust the guy and not screw him." At its peak, Jones' organization employed more than 70 people, including 18 baggers and 35 bundle dealers.

Liddy Jones recalled the time he owed Matthews $60,000 from a drug deal. "I kept calling Frank and asking him when we could meet so I could give him the money. Finally, he said to me, "Punk, why you calling me. If you broke, keep it, motherfucka!"

Rick Talley recalls an incident that also illustrates Matthews' blase attitude towards money: "I was working for a gentleman who owed Frank $40,000 for a certain product. Frank was supposed to meet us at a certain time and pick up the money, but he forgot about it. Four months later, Frank still had not come for the money. Finally my friend calls Frank and says, 'When are you going to pick up your money?' Frank told him, 'Keep it.'"

By 1971, Matthews' drug ring was so huge that he was working on getting 100 kilo drug shipments smuggled into the U.S. via Venezuela and the Corsican connection. One shipment, reportedly worth $150 million, boggles the imagination. The Corsicans had planned to pack heroin into World War II limpet mines and then send them across the Atlantic from Europe to Venezuela. When the mines arrived, Matthews would have had divers go into the harbor at night and retrieve the heroin. The Corsicans acknowledged that some of the mines would have been lost during the trans-Atlantic voyage, but they were confident they could still get $400 million worth of heroin smuggled successfully that way, or at least that was the plan. Matthews is believed to have put up $4 million to secure the deal.

Matthews' vision and shrewdness were abundantly evident in the way he handled his money. He hired Don Andrews, a professional financial consultant who also represented Mob figures, to help him invest his money in businesses and real estate that could serve as his front corporations and hide his money in overseas bank accounts. Matthews' business interests included the C and I Carpet Service at 140-2 Augustine Avenue, Far Rockaway, Queens, the Mattrack Enterprises Inc. at 1475 Fulton St., Brooklyn, and the Eastern Parkway Realty Corporation, also in Brooklyn. Matthews played the role of the successful entrepreneur, describing himself as a businessman with real estate investments.

Matthews also had business interests in locations outside New York City. A Durham, North Carolina businessman recalled how, in the early 1970s, Matthews inquired about buying property in the southern part of the county. "His movement into business real estate was quite extensive," the businessman explained. And there were rumors that Matthews was using a local bank for money laundering, although the authorities never found any evidence.

Matthews' business interests in Georgia were such that he bought a home in Atlanta and flew there on a weekly basis. He had real estate interests valued at $1.75 million in Georgia's Dekalb, Pike, Cherokee and Haralson counties. He purchased land with the expectation that the state of Georgia would buy it for the construction of a major highway. "Matthews paid bribes to get inside information," Callahan revealed. "He would have been a multimillionaire if he had not had to flee."

When Matthews traveled to Atlanta to see his associate and friend Nathaniel Elder and check on business, he would stop by the Playboy Club to visit with some of his girlfriends. "Frank liked blondes, and he would brag about blonde conquests when we had him on the wire," Garay recalled. "I remember him talking about how one of them had pissed him off and he had beaten her up pretty badly."

Interestingly, the authorities were able to determine that one of the investors in Matthews' C and I Carpet Service was the powerful Lucchese crime family Mafioso Anthony "Ducks" Corallo, an indication that Matthews' relationship with La Cosa Nostra was more complicated than generally portrayed. Corallo was given the nickname 'Tony Ducks" because of his ability to "duck" or avoid subpoenas and convictions. In May 1973, Corallo began serving as the undisputed head of the Lucchese crime family when its don, Carmine Tramunte, was sentenced to 15 years in federal prison.

That Matthews was investing his drug profits overseas is largely speculation because the laws in the 1970s were so weak that investigators could gain little evidence about money laundering. Ron Taylor, a retired special agent with the Intelligence Bureau of the Internal Revenue Service (IRS) who was involved with the Matthews investigation, said that until 1970 anybody could walk into a bank with a suitcase full of money and make a deposit, no questions asked. "Back then, there really were no investigative money laundering tools we could use," Taylor revealed.

Then with the passage of the Bank Secrecy Act in 1970, a person wanting to deposit more than $10,000 in a bank was required by law to fill out a special form. "Banks were slack in meeting that requirement," Taylor revealed. "Say a drug dealer wanted to deposit $100,000 in a bank, all he had to do was put $9,999 in ten different banks, and he could circumvent the requirement."

In the Matthews era, a drug dealer could simply hop a plane with a suitcase filled with cash and deposit the money in an offshore bank in the Cayman Islands, the Bahamas or some other money laundering haven, no questions asked, no paper trail to worry about. Remarkably, it was not until Congress passed the Money Laundering Act of 1986 that money laundering became a federal crime.

Taylor spent much time investigating the Frank Matthews connection to his aunt Marzella Steele Webb and trying to determine whether she was helping him launder money. "We were never able to find any evidence that money laundering was going on," said Taylor. "For that matter, we were never able to figure out what Matthews did with his money, even after he disappeared."

Matthews' generosity became legendary. Matthews was known to give away cars as well as money to people on the street. He would surprise friends by sending them packages containing thousands of dollars. One old timer from the Matthews era, who knew Black Caesar well, described him for writer Seth Ferranti, "He was a fair man. He didn't have all that ruthless shit with him, although it was there. Every year on Bedford Avenue, he gave a Cadillac. That's just how he was. He gave the keys, the paperwork, everything. He was a good dude."

Black Caesar's generosity extended to his offering of sage advice, especially to his homeboys back in Durham. Matthews and his boyhood friend Charles Clinton had gone down different paths in life since their youthful days in Durham, but they stayed in touch. When Frank came to town, he would look up his old friend. On one of those occasions, Matthews came to see Clinton while he was attending law school at North Carolina Central University in Durham. "I could still hear Frank outside the classroom window shouting in his high pitched voice. 'Charles Clinton, you come out here now,'" Clinton recalled with a laugh. "The professor said to me, 'I think someone is trying to get your attention.' I went outside to see Frank. I was going through some tough times, but Frank helped me spiritually as well as financially. We had a heart-to-heart conversation. He told me what he thought I was meant to be and suggested what I should do. I didn't know where he was most of the time, but he would always find me."

In 1971, Mickey Fortune, then a 16-year old kid, met a well-dressed, muscular and confident looking young black man who came to his sister's house in Brooklyn. The visitor had come to see Buster Watson, the boyfriend of Fortune's sister. Watson had grown up with famous boxer Floyd Patterson, and in the late 1950s, Patterson had asked Buster to join his entourage and help out as an assistant trainer. Easy going and talkative, Watson helped keep Patterson loose and relaxed. He was also in Patterson's corner for many of his memorable fights, including the loss to Swede Ingemar Johansson in June 1959, the fifth round stoppage of Johansson in the June 1960 rematch, the two brutal one round losses to Sonny Liston in 1961 and 1963, and the embarrassing KO loss to Muhammad Ali in 1965.

Watson and Patterson had a falling-out in the late 1960s after Buster objected to his friend trying to make a comeback in the ring. By then, big-time drug dealer Ed Bynum had recruited Buster into the drug game, and he became a major player himself. Big Ed was one of Matthews' close associates, and they put together some of the biggest drug deals of the late 1960s and early 1970s. In the summer of 1971 and winter of 1972, for example, Matthews and Bynum collaborated on four deliveries ranging in size from 75 to 152 kilos.

The young man who came to see Buster Watson was Frank Matthews. Fortune recalls Matthews driving up in a red Mark IV El Dorado, one of his favorite cars. In fact, Matthews liked the car so much that one of his nicknames was Mark IV. Fortune recalled, "He was dressed in a brightly colored Superfly style outfit. He got out of the car with a suitcase and went inside to see Buster. While they talked, I decided I would clean Matthews' car. After his meeting with Buster, Frank came out the house and saw me wiping down his car. He said, 'Young blood, you a good man.' He slipped me a $100 bill. That was the most money I had ever handled! Boy, was I happy… and impressed!"

Fortune recalls the second time that he met Matthews. He was at a club in Brooklyn that Matthews apparently owned and he recalled the club's name as either Mark 3 or 4 Ranch. "The bar was filled with people," Fortune recalled. "It looked like something out of a *Superfly* movie. I was mesmerized. Matthews spotted me and came over. He smiled and patted me on the back. He reached into his pocket, pulled out two one hundred dollar bills, handed them to me and walked away. He remembered me! That's the kind of guy he was... a street guy but very kind. Buster told me that Frank liked to give people opportunities. That was his nature. But if you didn't measure up, he would send you on your way."

Later Fortune would see Matthews at Buster's house after his arrest in January 1972 and before he jumped bail in July of that year. Watson told Fortune that he had helped Matthews raise the money for his bond. After Matthews jumped bail, Buster did not talk to Fortune about Matthews until one day... "It must have been 10 years later. I was with Buster when a dude came up to us and told Buster he had a message for him. They went to the side to talk. After the dude left, Buster told me what he said, 'I got a message from Frank,' the dude told Buster. 'He wants you to know that he's doing fine.'"

In the beginning, Matthews was low-key in style, but as his drug empire grew and the money poured in, he began playing the role of a Black Caesar. Decked out in his large sable mink coat and leather safari suits, the cigar-chomping drug kingpin could be seen moving about New York City in expensive cars and often with beautiful women. He paid cash for his fleet of Cadillac El Dorados and the other expensive cars he owned. He bought dozens of $300 suits at Jacques in Greenwich Village and enjoyed expensive restaurants, usually dining on the best cuts of steak. His favorite beverage was Piper Heidsieck, an expensive champagne.

Black Caesar was a regular patron of Harlem's most popular clubs and got the best seats to see Duke Ellington, Sammy Davis Jr. and Cab Calloway, or the latest hot act in town. "All the major players in the drug game hung out at many of the same bars in Brooklyn and Harlem— Under the Stairs on 96th, the Shalimar, Gold Lounge, the Oasis Lenox Lounge," Talley recalled. "A lot of them were like neighborhood bars. You didn't have the territorial thing like you had later with drug gangs."

Matthews used the Brownee's and the Tip Top Club as meeting places to arrange narcotics buys and deliveries. "Matthews also liked to hang out at the Club Baron at 132nd Street and Lenox Avenue," recalled Joseph Sapia, a former drug dealer from the Matthews era, who today is incarcerated in a New Jersey prison. The bar was co-owned by Walter Perry, a Matthews' business partner. Sapia used to hang out with Matthews and some dudes at a garage in Harlem and shoot the breeze. "I found Frank to be aloof but a good brother," Sapia recalled. "He never liked to be in one place too long."

Black Caesar had several pads all over New York City that he used as retreats, stash houses, and discreet places to meet his many girlfriends. Matthews' apartment at 3333 Henry Hudson Parkway, Riverdale, Bronx, was in the same building where up-and-coming fellow drug dealer Nicky Barnes occupied the penthouse. At the time, Barnes was not as big a name as Black Caesar but he would succeed Matthews as New York's biggest drug kingpin after Matthews jumped bail and disappeared. Known as Mr. Untouchable for his ability to avoid arrest, Barnes was played by Cuban Gooding Jr. in the movie *American Gangster*, which ostensibly portrayed Frank Lucas' life.

Mr. Untouchable organized the Council, a group that controlled a large part of New York City's drug trade in the mid-1970s. After his takedown in 1978 that sent him to jail for life without the possibility of parole, Barnes became one of the biggest snitches in U.S. history, helping put many of his associates behind bars, including his former associates Guy Fisher and Frank James. Barnes also helped to convict at least 50 more gangsters.

Eventually, Barnes was resentenced to 35 years and housed in a special Witness Security Unit at the federal prison in Otisville. He was released in August 1998.

Following his arrest, Barnes told his authorities that he had run into Frank Mathews in a New York City night club. He didn't recognize Matthews' face, Barnes recalled, but he did recognize his distinctive voice. Like Matthews, Mr. Untouchable disappeared after becoming a snitch, but in the Barnes' case, it was into the Federal Witness Protection Program.

In researching this book, the author interviewed a woman in Durham whose sister had dated Matthews. The source had met Barnes at a New York bar in the late 1960s while visiting her sister. She ran into Barnes one Sunday in 2011 at a church in Durham, North Carolina, the woman recalled, "Barnes must now be in his 70s, but I recognized him. He was well-dressed, wore aviator glasses and had a younger woman on his arm. Nicky had just entered the church, and I was in line in front of him. I looked around and was startled to see him. I blurted out, 'Nicky Barnes!' He looked at me and stammered, 'How do know me?' Someone in front of me said something and I turned around. When I turned around again, Nicky and his lady friend were gone. I have never seen him again, but I knew that was him." If the story is true, it is ironic that Nicky Barnes would be hiding out in Frank Matthews' home town.

In the early 1970s, Frank Matthews fell for Cheryl Denise Brown, a beautiful woman about six years younger than Frank. Brown's parents were middle-class teachers from Queens, and given the backgrounds of Cheryl and Frank, it seemed like an unlikely romance. Matthews and Brown may have looked as if they had nothing in common, but, as they say, opposites do attract. "She was in a nightclub one night when Frank came in," said Roger Garay. "Cheryl was apparently blown away by Frank—his charisma, money, car. Then it was Cheryl and Frank...constant companions. I'm sure Barbara Hinton eventually found out about her, and even knew about her, but it apparently didn't affect her relationship with Frank."

Sources who knew Brown say the young woman left a memorable impression. "She was stunning and very attractive," Clinton recalled. "She had a Halley Barryesque look and an air about her." Garay added some details, "She was beautiful... well built... great body."

Matthews was intelligent in most matters, but it was a different story when it came to drugs. He broke the cardinal rule that all drug kingpins should follow: do not sample your product. It appears Matthews became a cocaine abuser, maybe even an addict. In the late 1960s and early 1970s, the Cubans, not the Colombians, mainly controlled the supply of cocaine to the U.S. from Latin America, and Matthews had easy access to what was called the "Champagne of Drugs" through his Miami Cuban connection. Matthews met George Ramos, a young, ambitious Cuban-American gangster from Miami who was attracted to Matthews' power and money. Ramos, through his connection to his godfather, Miguel Garcia, was soon supplying Matthews with all the cocaine he wanted.

According to Donald Goddard, author of *Easy Money* that chronicles the Matthews-Ramos relationship: "By the autumn of 1972, Matthews showed the classic symptoms of chronic cocaine abuse, shuffling between extremes of euphoria and irritability in an almost continuous macho-delusional power trip." This helps explain Matthews' frequent irrational behavior—his nonchalance and openness in the way he handled drug deals and his erratic driving and high speed dashes through the city that scared the shit out of his passengers.

After the authorities had Matthews' house bugged, they heard Barbara Hinton on the wire admonishing Matthews for his abuse of cocaine. Matthews may have been risking his health and increasing his chances of going to any early grave, according to William Callahan, a retired federal prosecutor who investigated Matthews. "During the course of our investigation, we learned that he had a rapid irregular heartbeat," Callahan revealed. "So by abusing cocaine Matthews was risking his health."

Like many of the big players in the drug game, Black Caesar loved the Las Vegas scene, and he traveled there often to gamble and party. Once Nevada legalized gambling, La Cosa Nostra moved into Las Vegas, and mobsters like Benjamin Siegel and Meyer Lansky began building casinos. The millions of dollars the Mafia made from the casino gambling profits were legitimate, but they also had an illegal operation called "The Skim" that involved taking money from the casinos' money counting rooms before they could be taxed. Since there was no record of the money, the Mafia did not have to account for it to the IRS. The Mob-owned casinos were also suspected of running money-laundering operations for both their own members and for other gangsters.

"We heard Frank would take duffel bags full of cash to a casino and give them to a cashier," Callahan said. "The casino would take 15 to 18 percent for laundering his money."

Frank Matthews loved to stay at the Sands, in the 1970s, one of Las Vegas' most popular venues. In 1956, the Sands became the seventh hotel to open on the strip. Some of the greatest names in the entertainment industry began performing at the legendary Sands showroom, the Copa Room, named after the famous Copacabana Club in New York City. Frank Sinatra and Rat Pack members Dean Martin and Sammy Davis Jr. performed there, as did such luminaries as Tony Bennett, Louis Armstrong and Marlene Dietrich.

Freddie Myers, who was known on the street as New York Freddie, was one of the biggest Harlem drug dealers in the 1970s, making, according to press reports, about $9 million a week from drug trafficking. Myers spent time with Black Caesar at the Sands around New Year's 1969. New York Freddie had been released from prison the year before and had made some money dealing on the streets. He decided to treat himself to a trip to Las Vegas.

In the 2007 documentary *Kingpins: The Freddie Myers Story*, Myers told director Jay Brooks how he met Matthews and how his friendship with the drug kingpin developed: "I didn't know Frank at the time but he was sitting next to me on the plane. He spotted my watch. It was blue and had a diamond studded "F" where the 12 should have been. Frank asked me if he could see my watch. I let him look at it. He examined it and said: 'Do you want to sell it?' I went ego on him and said: 'What you mean sell my watch? I'm New York Freddie, nigga. I'm not going to sell it to you or anybody else.' Frank gave me a little grin and didn't say anything.

"When we got to Las Vegas, he had a limousine waiting for him and offered me a ride to my hotel. Then he said: 'Why don't you come with me. I'm staying at the Sands.' I did that. He had both Frank Sinatra's and Sammy Davis, Jr.'s private suites. I went with him to the casino and saw him drop $15,000 in a couple of seconds. I said to myself: 'Who is this guy?' When we got back to the room, he ordered some expensive liquor from room service. In a couple of minutes I heard a knock at the door. I thought it was room service, but it was a blond and a redhead. We immediately got busy. I got the blond and Frank got the redhead. After we were through, he pulled out $3,500 and gave it to the girls. I said to him: 'You going to give them all that money for a piece of pussy?' So I went and got some more. This time, he fucked the red head and I had the blond. We had a lot of fun together and did a lot of drugs together."

Black Cesar also liked New York Freddie's style and the way he dressed and would go with New York Freddie on shopping sprees where they would spend $20,000 to $30,000 on clothes in a day. Matthews also took Myers to the Ponderosa where he saw a room full of women bagging heroin. "I said to Frank: 'How long have they been working?'" Myers recalled. "Frank said: 'All week.' I asked how much dope were they gonna bag? He said 85 keys. I said to Frank: 'That's a lot of work. You a bad motherfucka. I've never seen 86 keys of dope.'"

Friends and associates who partied with Matthews in Las Vegas say he would bring suitcases full of money with him. "We would leave the suitcases in the hotel room while we went out to gamble and have a good time," Liddy Jones recalled. "Nobody would watch the suitcases, but nothing was ever stolen." Jones said Frank brought the money in suitcases to Las Vegas so it could be laundered, although he never actually saw Matthews make a laundering deal.

Matthews lost money in the casino most of the time, hundreds of thousands of dollars, not pocket change, in fact. According to Callahan, "Matthews was a craps junkie. He would spend almost every minute of the day at the Sands' crap tables. He would play with a fist full of money and the crowd would cheer him on."

Black Caesar also liked to play baccarat, according to Reggie Collins (aka Clarence Gardner), a former drug dealer from the Matthews' era who is currently incarcerated in Baldwin State Prison in Hardwick, Georgia. "Frank called me Baseball," Collins explained. "I'd seen Frank around, but met him for the first time at the 1969 Penn Relays in Philadelphia. He was with Fat Ty Palmer. I went to Las Vegas three or four time with Frank. He loved the Sands. One time, I saw him lose $50,000 at the baccarat table. I suspected Frank was money laundering the losses, but he never talked about it."

Former big-time drug dealer Courtney Brown recalls the time in the early 1970s when he and his partner Eddie Jackson bumped into Matthews at a Las Vegas casino. "This black guy is standing at the table and gambling with a handful of money. Eddie sees him and asks him what is he betting on? The brother says, 'I'm betting against the house.' I say, 'Yo, homey, where you from? He says, 'I'm from New York and my name is Frank Matthews.' We learned we had some mutual friends." Courtney Brown and Eddie Jackson oversaw a heroin ring in Detroit between 1970 and 1975 that grossed several million dollars.

Both law enforcement and Matthews' associates say Black Caesar was extremely popular in Las Vegas. "He was really generous," Garay explained. "Frank would give the help in the bathrooms $100 for simply handing him a towel." Jones recalls the time he was walking with Mathews through the Sands Hotel and people were yelling, "Frank, Frank! Hey, Frank!" Jones looked around to see if Old Blues was there. "They were calling out Frank so much I thought they were calling out Frank Sinatra's name," Jones said with a laugh.

Matthews was a big fan of Muhammad Ali, and he loved to attend his boxing matches in Las Vegas as well as in other big cities. Black Caesar was at Madison Square Gardens in 1971 when Ali fought Frazier for Frazier's heavyweight title belt and lost in a thrilling fight. The authorities were there, too, watching Black Caesar's every move.

On June 26, 1972, Matthews was in Las Vegas for the second Ali-Quarry fight. The FBI also came to conduct surveillance at the Sands and the Convention Center where the fight was being held. The FBI had come to investigate possible money-laundering schemes involving Las Vegas casinos and banking institutions in the Bahamas.

The fight, one of the biggest in years, drew 8,579 paid spectators, a Nevada record. In all, more than 39 million viewers watched Muhammad

Ali, a 5-to -1 favorite, defeat Quarry by a TKO in the seventh round. Interestingly, in the post-fight interview, Ali made a pitch for friend Major Coxson and his campaign for Mayor of Camden, New Jersey, dedicating the fight to "the next mayor of Camden, New Jersey, Mayor Coxson."

Liddy Jones came to Las Vegas with Pop Darby, another close Matthews' friend and associate, at Matthews' invitation, and they stayed together at the Sands. The two had come to attend a special meeting organized by Matthews of major black drug dealers from along the Eastern Seaboard. It was not the first such Matthews sponsored meeting. In October 1971 he called a meeting of black and Hispanic drug lords and financiers in Atlanta to discuss ways to improve the distribution of heroin and cocaine and to discuss important issues relating to La Cosa Nostra.

The ambitious Black Caesar was always looking for ways to expand his business and make himself—as well as the drug trade—more independent of the white Mafia. More than 40 representatives came for the second meeting in Las Vegas. The DEA knew about the meeting and came to Atlanta as well. "When we began checking out the license plates and the intelligence on who was in attendance, we could see it was meeting of the Who's Who of black organized crime," recalled Gerard Miller, the agent who headed the DEA's Matthews investigation. "Matthews was the reason they came. At the time he really was the country's biggest black kingpin."

The gathering in Las Vegas decided that they should work more closely with the Corsicans and Cubans in Miami and Latin America so as to protect themselves against a possible rupture in smuggling that would result from their relationship with La Cosa Nostra contacts or the breakup of its French Connection. By now the French Connection had collapsed. Turkey had banned opium production, and Amsterdam had replaced Marseille as the center of European heroin production. Other trafficking groups were now rising to compete with the Mafia for heroin dollars in New York City and throughout the U.S. Cocaine, however, was a different story. The meeting agreed to diversify more into cocaine since large supplies of the drug were available.

Once the meeting ended, it was time to relax. Later, at the post-fight Ali-Quarry interview, Liddy jumped into the ring to get close to Ali. Heavyweight challenger George Foreman got into the ring as well and started talking trash with The Greatest. Jones got angry and started yelling at Foreman. "Punk, you can't even beat me. What the fuck are you talking about!"

Liddy's run-in with George Foreman caught the attention of security, and they got the police. "The cops were going to lock me up," Liddy recalled. "When they were about to take me out the door, Frank pulled the lieutenant over and said something to him. The lieutenant listened and then told his men to let me go. Frank got me out of that jam."

By this time, Matthews was getting into a jam himself with the law. The Federal Government had begun an investigation that would culminate in Las Vegas.

# FIVE

# THE INVESTIGATION BEGINS

*"I did not like him the first time I saw him," Kowalski recalled. "He was loud and flashy, drove fancy cars and never seemed to go to work."*
**Joe Kowalski, NYPD detective**

B Y 1970, FRANK "Black Caesar" Matthews was the biggest drug kingpin in the U.S. He came to the big city as an African-American in his early 20s and a country boy from the rural South, but he had managed to circumvent the Italian Mafia and make a connection to a major narcotics source in Venezuela. It was a development almost unheard of in the American underworld at the time. Leslie Ike Atkinson, a drug kingpin who smuggled millions of dollars of heroin from Bangkok to the U.S. via a connection to the Golden Triangle, was the only other brother kingpin who could lay claim to such an accomplishment.

As Black Caesar worked hard to set up his organization along the Eastern Seaboard, he showed himself to be a master strategist and tactician with a great a sense of the big picture and of what he needed to do to become successful. "Here was a young black guy from the South who knew how to oversee transportation, set up heroin manufacturing facilities, maintain security, launder money, and so on," explained Al Bradley (aka Al Profit), co-director and the co-producer of the documentary *The Frank Matthews Story.* "It's amazing to see what he did as a self-made man and how he built a criminal empire on his own. I think the only people in organized crime history comparable to Matthews are Lucky Luciano and Pablo Escobar."

Matthews rose to the top quietly but he quickly became a legend in the hood. Still, law enforcement did not have a clue who he was. "In 1970, Matthews' name did not appear on any of the major criminal violators lists kept by the authorities," said William Callahan, a U.S. government attorney who investigated Matthews. "He was a non-entity."

That is because Matthews kept a low profile when he started out in the drug game. Beginning in May 1968, Matthews, his common law wife and three kids moved to an apartment 4B at 130 Clarkson Avenue in a peaceful middle-class Brooklyn neighborhood. When people asked him what he did for a living, Matthews looked them in the eye and said, "I'm in real estate."

Black Caesar's criminal life might not have come to law enforcement's attention if it had not been for some bad luck. Black Caesar did not know it, but one of his neighbors at 130 Clarkson Avenue was a veteran of the New York Police Department named Joe Kowalski. "My (astrological) sign is Virgo and we tend to be nosey people," Kowalski explained. "That was bad news for Frank Matthews."

Kowalski joined the NYPD on October 1, 1962, and worked in uniform duty in New York Police Department's (NYPD) 84th Precinct before being assigned to its Central Investigation Bureau (CIB). According to one NYPD report, Kowalski's assignment to the CIB was predicated on his knowledge and experience as a former telephone company employee and the fact that he had "continually performed his duties with the Command in an efficient and highly commendable manner."

Observing Matthews' movements for several months, Kowalski found it strange that while his neighbor looked as if he had money, he exhibited no visible means of support. "I did not like him the first time I saw him," Kowalski recalled. "He was loud and flashy, drove fancy cars and never seemed to go to work."

Kowalski recalled the day he was on the elevator for the first time with Matthews and one of his associates. Always a cop, Kowalski thought it would be a good opportunity to size up the suspicious neighbor. The detective noted, "The 5' 8" or 5' 9" tall Matthews was muscular, from 180 to 190 pounds, and appeared to be in his mid 20s. He had short-cropped hair, but his clothes could have made him stand out in a pitch-black room. He wore a white mink coat and fashionable platform shoes and he sparkled with jewelry.

"Matthews was talking in a soft voice to his associate when suddenly he exploded, 'That Guinea bastard! That son-of-a-bitch. Who does he think he is? If I had a gun, I'd blow him away!'" Watching Matthews spew venom, Kowalski had no doubt the gangster was capable of doing just that.

While suspicious of the new neighbor, Kowalski did not want to alert his superiors until he had enough evidence proving Matthews was involved with some kind of criminal activity, so he conducted his investigation while off duty. Kowalski had access to the investigative tools of the CIB and he quietly and unofficially began to look into Frank Matthews' background. His investigation revealed that neither Frank Matthews nor Barbara Hinton had a criminal record.

The detective further learned that Matthews had a gold Cadillac registered to a company called Mattrank Enterprises, Inc., at 1475 Fulton Street in Brooklyn. Matthews had no broker's license, and records contained no listing for Mattrank Enterprises, Inc. Matthews had bought a 1970 Cadillac, and when Kowalski did a check of the car registration, he found out that, for some strange reason, it was registered to a Philadelphia, Pennsylvania address. Meanwhile, Barbara Hinton was driving an expensive green 1970 Cadillac El Dorado registered in her name.

In the months after Matthews moved in, the parking lot at the Clarkson apartment building began to look like a luxury car sales lot filled with high-priced Mercedes, Mercuries, Cadillacs and Buicks. People began streaming into the building at all hours of the day to see the residents in 4B. The visitors were black and as flashy and loud as Matthews. They would block the driveways with their cars and park in other people's parking spaces. Many of them carried paper bags that looked as if they might contain money.

Looking out his apartment window, Kowalski would sometimes see black men strategically located around the apartment building. The detective knew from his experience that this kind of activity was a good sign a drug buy was going down.

Kowalski began keeping the visitors under surveillance. He took down license plate numbers and did background checks, using NYPD resources. He put the license plate numbers through the Motor Vehicles database and was not surprised to learn that many of the cars were registered to known drug dealers living not just in the Big Apple but in cities throughout the east, midwest and the south, including Durham, a small town in North Carolina. There was Albert Phillip Wylie, a male negro, 35-40 years old, from Baltimore, who worked for James Westcott, a major drug trafficker in the city. An "unknown negro" appeared to drive a car registered to Nathaniel Elder, a major trafficker in narcotics who "has been a target of the federal authorities in the Atlanta, Georgia area." Another unknown "male negro" visitor, 35-40 years, drove a 1971 Cadillac Eldorado registered to Scarvey McCargo, a major trafficker from New Haven, Connecticut.

Kowalski began checking the telephone records of Frank Matthews and discovered that he was in contact with individuals whom the Bureau of Narcotics and Dangerous Drugs (BNDD), the DEA's predecessor, had identified as major narcotics violators. They were located all over the eastern U.S. and included some notorious big time dealers, such as James Craven (Cincinnati, Ohio), James Olive Rowland (Durham, North Carolina) and Shelby Cotton (Chicago, Illinois).

Obsessed with finding out more about Matthews, Kowalski began keeping a detailed log of the suspect's activities. "I took a lot of chances," Kowalski conceded. "When I thought Matthews wasn't around, I'd go to the garage and look into his car. I'd test his car door; it was always locked, but I'd see an attaché case in the back seat. Matthews seemed to be really careless."

One day in February 1971, Kowalski saw Matthews acting suspiciously in the garage area of the apartment complex. He searched the area when no one was around but found nothing. A few days later, he did another search near Matthews's car and found a small silver foil package wrapped in wax paper and hidden within the padding placed around a support pole. It contained one ounce of white powder.

More searching uncovered another one-ounce package of white powder, wrapped in wax paper. Kowalski took samples of both packages back to the NYPD headquarters where he had them tested at the police lab. The powder was found to be cocaine of good quality. Although the discovery could not have gotten Matthews arrested, Kowalski knew he was onto something criminal.

The detective's investigation went on for months as he continued to gather a small mountain of information. Finally, he decided it was time to submit a detailed report of his findings to his superiors. In his report, Kowalski noted that while Matthews' criminal record indicated that he had no narcotics arrests, a check with federal authorities revealed that the "subject was often mentioned in several unrelated and out-of-state investigations." It was further learned that Frank Matthews was considered extremely dangerous and suspected of several criminal homicides occurring in the past." Kowalski's supervisor read his report and told him, "You did a wonderful job, Joe, but this case is too big for us. We are going to give it to the New York Joint Drug Task Force."

Case 459, as the Matthews investigation became known, was assigned to Group 12 of the New York Joint Task Force. The Joint Task Force was created on February 2, 1970, when John V. Lindsey (New York City Mayor), Nelson Rockefeller (Governor of New York), and John Mitchell (U.S. Attorney General) signed an agreement to contribute personnel to a taskforce that would aggressively attack the New York City narcotics problem.

Group 12 was a sub group within the Task Force. William Callahan, a special attorney with ODALE, was selected to coordinate the federal government's investigation of Frank Matthews. In reviewing Callahan's background it is evident that he was well qualified to be the investigative attorney on the case. His father had been head of the Manhattan homicide squad and Callahan, himself, had spent seven years defending criminals before he went to prosecuting them. Callahan also had close ties to the Nixon administration. "Uncle Sam was fully committed to using all of its resources to take Frank Matthews down," Callahan explained.

Group 12 was headed by Gerard Miller, a narcotics agent who had 20 years of experience working on organized crime cases in Chicago, Detroit and Miami. Early in his career, Miller had voluntarily spent time in prison to learn more about the kind of men he would be dealing with in law enforcement. Miller came to the Joint Task Force from Miami where he had been with Operation Eagle, the first successful takedown of Cuban traffickers in Florida. Kowalski was assigned to Group 12 Task Force to aid in its continuing investigation and to add manpower when needed.

The investigation's objective was to collect evidence that could prove Matthews was involved in a conspiracy to transport and sell narcotics. To do that, the Task Force would have to search through reams of material—intelligence data, polygraphs, motion picture files and recorded transcripts of conversations and put together bits and pieces of information that would document the structure and activities of the criminal organization it identified as the Frank Matthews Syndicate.

The investigation of Matthews began at a time when the U.S. was intensifying its efforts to combat international drug trafficking. In July 1971, President Richard Nixon identified what became known as the War on Drugs and declared drug abuse to be "Public Enemy Number One." Nixon warned Congress that drug addiction had "the dimensions of a national emergency," and he asked Congress for an initial $84 million in funds for what would be short term emergency measures. In January 1972, the President established the Office of Drug Abuse Law Enforcement (ODALE), a U.S. Justice Department initiative that was chiefly a tool for the federal government to assist local government in enforcing drug laws and encouraging drug addicts to undergo rehabilitation. The following year, the President created the Drug Enforcement Administration (DEA), the successor agency to the BNDD, to coordinate the illicit drug fighting efforts of all the agencies.

Reading through Kowalski's report of the Matthews investigation, Miller was astonished to learn that such a major drug dealer had slipped under law enforcement's radar. But how could a young black man in his 20s be trafficking in at least 21 states? Could a black drug dealer get that big in the drug trade when the only arrest he had on his rap sheet was for stealing chickens? Miller's respect for Matthews as a worthy adversary only got greater as the investigation progressed. Today, Miller says with a laugh, "I hate to say it, but Frank was ahead of us from the beginning."

The Frank Matthews' investigation was not an easy one to pursue. Group 12 had not yet proven itself and was under great pressure to show results. Miller felt the investigation would help the Joint Task Force make its mark, but his bosses were skeptical. They were reluctant to assign precious resources to the investigation, so Miller would have to use the available manpower and equipment wisely.

Group 12 had to work long hours without overtime and pay their own expenses for gas and supplies. Stretched so thin at times, they often had to spend days on surveillance huddled up in their cars and using a nearby hotel to wash up. Money was so tight, in fact, that Group 12 members chipped in to pay for a month's rent on a vacant first floor apartment building opposite 130 Clarkson that they wanted to use for surveillance.

The brass put the Group 12 under the gun. It would have about three months to produce something significant from the investigation, but they would have to do it without arresting anybody or interfering with any transaction they might observe. Three months? Not much time to nail a big-time gangster like Matthews. To put a solid drug conspiracy case together actually required months, sometimes years of investigation.

As Miller explained the challenge, "They (Group 12) were too few to be discreet, particularly on any surveillance." To have followed Black Caesar and his visitors and passengers without tipping its hand the Group 12 would have needed six cars at least, with two men assigned to each car. Miller could rarely afford the luxury of even using half that many men at a time. Just by staying home, Matthews immobilized half of Group 12's manpower.

Black Caesar was a night owl, so Group12 investigators would have to be up at all hours of the night. Garay gave Black Caesar a nickname, "The Bat," because it seemed Matthews only came out at night.

Still, Group 12 tried to make the best of a tough situation. At times, they got creative. Donald Goddard, author of *Easy Money*, described how they tried to make up for the shortage of surveillance vehicles: "They equipped one car for night-time duty with a rheostat control on the headlights. By varying the brightness and occasionally switching one or the other of them altogether, they hoped to pass themselves off as several different cars in Matthews' rearview mirror."

At a May 25, 1971 meeting of the Joint Task Force and the NYPD's Organized Crime Section, a number of steps were taken to get the Matthews investigation rolling. The court authorized wiretaps of Matthews' phones, and Group 12 conducted a complete survey of all his telephone toll activity. The first wiretap was issued on June 27, 1972, and extended the following month on August 24, 1972, when the court granted a second wiretap. Garay told the court that the investigation needed a second wiretap because Matthews' evasive tactics made it tough to obtain additional information for the case through conventional surveillance and investigation. The second wiretap continued in operation until September 22, 1972. Wiretapping Matthews' operation, however, was not an easy task. Matthews operated in 21 states and made dozens of calls. There were so many wiretapped recorded conversions, in fact, that the Group 12 became overwhelmed in checking them out.

Eventually, Group 12 learned that Matthews knew his phones were being wiretapped—or at least suspected it—when one day on the wire Matthews warned Beckwith about talking too much. "They got cat's eyes." In referring to law enforcement, Matthews warned Beckwith: "They can see in the dark."

Group 12 began collecting some interesting information. He was building a house on Staten Island and he intended to move his family there. The house was located on Buttonwood Road at either number 5 or 9 in the exclusive Staten Island neighborhood of Todt Hill. On June 1, 1971, Detective Joe Kowalski and another New York State police investigator surveyed the area around Matthews' future home in Todt Hill to determine the kind of manpower and equipment the Group 12 would need to conduct surveillance.

They noticed that the house across the street (Buttonwood 10) from the subject had the name Lucchese on the mail box. More investigations revealed that the residents at 10 Buttonwood were related to Tommy Three Finger Lucchese, the powerful La Cosa Nostra boss who had died of a brain tumor in 1967.

Group 12 investigators were put in touch with an employee of Piedmont Airlines who claimed that stewardesses from the airline were being used to transport narcotics for Matthews. The informant also said that narcotics were being supplied by Lakewood Food, Inc., which provided food services for Piedmont, Alleghany and United Airlines. Kowalski revealed how he had looked into one of Matthews' autos and had seen material for Alleghany Airlines on the front seat. Group 12 eventually learned that Matthews employed several stewardesses and was paying them $1000 a month for each shipment of heroin they carried. The stewardess would pick up the packages at an airport locker, pack it in her airline flight bag and leave it at another airport locker upon arrival.

Although at this point, Group 12 had uncovered evidence showing that Matthews was not your typical punk street drug dealer, they still conservatively estimated that he was trafficking a paltry 50 kilograms of heroin per month. Group 12, however, had to revise this figure upwards as they learned more about the amazing Black Caesar.

Matthews appeared to be popular on the street, from what Group 12 could gather, but an anonymous letter showed that not everybody liked Black Caesar. Received on February 10, 1971, by the FBI office in Atlanta, Georgia, the letter writer signed himself Aquarius and provided a wealth of detailed information about Matthews and his principal associates, including residences, aliases, addresses, phone numbers and the cities and states where they had their cars registered. "This information proved to be 100 percent accurate, so it had to be written by somebody close to Matthews," explained Jack Rawald, Group 12's Deputy Supervisor.

Black Caesar must have really pissed off somebody because there was no offer to snitch for money.

The Atlanta letter sparked an investigation in Georgia that revealed Matthews had real estate interests in the state valued at $1.7 million.

The kingpin had shrewdly bought several parcels of land that promised to make him a fortune. Somehow Matthews was one of the few people who knew that a new highway was being proposed and that it would go directly through the property he had bought. "We heard rumors that Matthews paid big bribes to learn what property the highway was going through," Callahan revealed. "The purchase could have made Matthews a multi, multi-millionaire if he hadn't got into trouble with the law."

As the investigation proceeded and grew in scope, other BNDD offices, especially the one in Greensboro, North Carolina, got involved in the investigation. When BNDD agent Rich Broughton went to work at the Greensboro office in March 1971, there was no case file on Frank Matthews. That changed, however, when a pharmacist in Roxboro, North Carolina contacted the Greensboro office with some interesting information. A black man from Durham had come to the pharmacy to see if he could buy a 50 gallon drum of quinine and have it shipped to New York City. The pharmacist suspected illegal drugs were involved because he knew quinine was used to cut heroin.

"We found out the customer was using an alias and that he was from Durham (North Carolina)," Broughton recalled. "So we called the Durham Police Department to see if they could help us. We learned the man's name was Frank Matthews. We called the BNDD office in New York City, but they had little information on him and were not interested in pursuing the matter. We never did find out why Matthews himself had gone to Roxboro to buy quinine, but in not following up, we had lost an opportunity."

The level of interest in Matthews changed when the Joint Task Force took over the Matthews investigation. The BNDD's Greensboro Office opened a file on Matthews and began collecting intelligence. The BNDD leaned that Matthews visited Durham often and stayed at Aunt Marzella's house. With the help of the Durham police, the BNDD put the aunt's house under surveillance. "We used a beat up old jalopy and had one of local black police officers drive it so as not attract suspicion," Broughton recalled. "We had intelligence revealing that Miller was using

Durham banks to launder money, and we suspected Marzella was helping him." We didn't think Marzella was involved in heroin smuggling, though, because her husband was a Durham City police officer."

The BNDD also pumped local informants for information. "Matthews' name came up a lot in conversations, but we could not pin down the names of any customers he had in the Durham area," Broughton recalled. "We learned that a lot of heroin was coming into North Carolina, but it was coming in from Ike Atkinson's organization and not from Matthews."The more evidence Group 12 uncovered, the more it became necessary to bring the expertise and help of other federal and international agencies. The Bureau of Alcohol, Tobacco and Firearms (ATF) began investigating the Miami area about a case involving aliens who were being used as couriers for the Matthews' organization. Group 12 notified the IRS and its Narcotics Trafficking Program about assigning a team of IRS agents to work closely with the Matthews' prosecution and Group 12.The mammoth size of Matthews' organization was evident in the fact that investors had to request information about Black Caesar from more than a dozen IRS district offices, coast to coast. The joint effort eventually led to the location and eventual seizure of assets belonging to Matthews, including several real estate properties.

Group 12 also used Interpol to determine the driver of a late model foreign car whose passenger had delivered a large green cellophane package to Matthews' Clarkson address. The continued observation of Clarkson Avenue and Brownies Bar and other known drug dealer hangouts produced the names and addresses of other narcotics offenders linked to Matthews. Moreover, through this surveillance, the authorities were able to observe Elder and Matthews receiving packages from a car trunk, entering Matthews Clarkson Avenue apartment, exiting with a package and going to Brownie's Bar to meet Gattis Hinton.

Given Group 12's limitations, it wasn't too long before Matthews spotted the surveillance. Roger Garay recalled the challenges once this happened. "Admittedly, this surveillance stuff was new to me. After all, I was working in Brooklyn's 66th Precinct just a few months before. Our team was under strict instructions from our supervisors, Jerry Miller and Bill Rawald, not to get burned. Miller was always worried that we would jump Matthews during a suspected drug transaction, so he often warned us, 'Screw up and you're back in uniform.' We would stay back several blocks and wait for Matthews to appear. Then all of a sudden there he was—driving like a madman. He knew we were tailing him, so he attempted to draw out our surveillance vehicles. When Matthews reached a speed of 85 to 90 miles an hour, we dropped off of him. After all, speed kills."

Garay recalled one incident that could have put him back in uniform within hours. "We were tailing Matthews in Harlem during the daytime. He was driving at a very slow speed. My partner, Jack Dworsak, was hidden in a big flower box positioned on top of our surveillance car. I tried to stay back, but because of the traffic, I found myself directly behind Matthews' Cadillac.

"Then Matthews suddenly stopped his car. Maybe he spotted us. Meanwhile, I'm looking ahead and to the sides, staying in touch with Jack in the box when all of a sudden, I jam on the brakes to avoid a collision with Frank's car. That caused Jack to fly out of the box and fall across the hood of the car and land on the roadway.

"Jack is laid out there on the street. I get out of the car. Frank gets out of his car and starts yelling at me for hitting the 'pedestrian.'

"I played the role. I picked Jack up and profusely apologized to him. 'Shit,' said Matthews, 'Not a goddamn cop around when you need one.' Then Frank drove away, laughing. We didn't talk about this faux pas for several days, fearing that the wiretap monitors would hear about a surveillance team 'made' by Matthews. We survived and didn't have to go back to the bag. That's police jargon for wearing a uniform."

Black Caesar was obviously having fun. It was as if he had a green light to break every traffic rule on the books. He would tear down a one-way street going in the opposite direction, jump red lights, suddenly do a U-turn and blast away in the opposite direction.

Matthews' driving was such that he would make his homies and associates queasy when they got in the car with him. "One time I took a cab and met Frank in Brooklyn," explained Donald Keno, who was a lieutenant of Ray Daniels aka Dutch Shultz, one of Black Caesar's biggest customers. "He gave me a package of like five keys, all wrapped up. He offered to drive me back. During the ride he was driving extremely fast. We ran a couple of traffic lights and I get scared. He was driving a green convertible Cadillac and he scared the shit out of me. I said (to Frank), 'Maybe I should take a cab. I'm holding five keys and any minute the cops are going to stop us.' He just laughed."

Was Frank high on cocaine or merely sticking it to Group 12? "Who knows," Garay said. "It didn't really matter. We knew it was futile to follow him." Miller added, "He didn't seem to fear anything." The agents were amazed at how ballsy Matthews could get at times. Garay recalled, "He'd go to Harlem and we'd hear that that Frank would open up his trunk in broad daylight, take out a couple of keys and give them to somebody."

Garay recalls another incident that made him wonder if Matthews knew something Group 12 didn't. "It was really frustrating," Garay recalled. "We were watching his Clarkson (Avenue) apartment from across the street. A white Bentley pulled up in front of the building. Could you imagine that? A white Bentley in Brooklyn. It was three in the morning. Matthews came outside. The guy in the white Bentley takes out a kilo from his car and throws it to Matthews, who puts it into the trunk of his car. Matthews jumps in his El Dorado and takes off. We follow him. It's as if he knew we were following him. We lose him at 90 mph. We later learned that he had ended up at one of his apartments near the Kennedy airport."

Was the apparent recklessness really the result of his cocaine use, or did he know something his pursuers didn't? Was corruption involved and was Matthews protected?

Corruption was widespread in New York City law enforcement in the Matthews era, and no law enforcement agency was immune. In December 1968, for instance, the *New York Times* reported that 32 agents from the Federal Bureau of Narcotics (FBN), a predecessor of the BNDD and the DEA, had resigned after the FBN had launched an investigation in August 1967. The U.S. Attorney General Ramsey Clark told the press that the investigation had uncovered significant corruption that involved "the illegally selling and buying of drugs, retaining confiscated contraband for personal use and sale, taking money meant for informants and failing to enforce the law."

In some instances, the dirty agents acted like mobsters. The authorities, for example, arrested two agents in 1967 and indicted them in August on conspiracy to use thousands of dollars in seized and counterfeit bills to buy narcotics for sale on the illegal market.

Like the federal crime-fighting agencies, the NYPD was not immune from the drug trade-related corruption. Between 1969 and 1972, NYPD detectives stole approximately 400 pounds of heroin and cocaine with a half-million dollars from the NYPD property office in Lower Manhattan. The theft, known as the "French Connection Theft," the biggest corruption scandal in NYPD history, was popularized by the 1972 Academy Award winning movie *The French Connection*. Only a small percentage of that amount was ever recovered.

Matthews did not talk or brag about whom he had on his payroll, but many sources believe he had his hooks dug deep into New York City law enforcement. As one retired drug dealer from that era explained, "Every major drug dealer during Frank's era had some cops on their payroll." One DEA report revealed that, on one occasion, a worker at one Matthews' heroin processing mills died. When the police showed up at the front door, Matthews went outside to talk to them. After a few minutes they were gone. Nothing further happened as a result of the incident and it was business as usual for the processing mill.

Group 12's perseverance, however, was beginning to pay off. One day, Garay and Dworzak spotted Matthews in a new Cadillac and followed him to 101 East 56th Street in Brooklyn. Matthews got out of the car and looked at the cars lining the block in front of the building. He went into a rage and didn't calm down until a couple of men came out of the building and moved their cars. The men followed Matthews into the building. Putting the location under surveillance, Group 12 observed the arrival of busloads of people who would then go into the building

When Group 12 decided to investigate the building on East 56th Street, they later learned it was known to the Matthews organization as the OK Corral. Plywood buttressed all of the building's windows, so it was impossible to see inside. Garay and Dworsak decided to start a private paint company, the J and R Paint Company, which would allow them to pose as contractors. They then devised a scheme where they would pull up to the building during the daytime and act as if they were doing a color plan for painting the building.

"We raised a ladder to one of the windows and saw that the inside plywood was not quite up to the top of the window," Garay recalled. "Jack actually started to paint the outside window with the most horrible green paint that you could imagine. All we wanted to do was to look like painters so we could try to find out what was going on inside. Unfortunately, we couldn't see into the premises, so our painting company was dissolved that day without incident."

It was another frustrating experience for Group 12 investigators. Matthews' organization continued to feed the drug habit of America and make millions of dollars doing it. But Group 12 investigators knew that they were closing in. They could smell it. They could feel it. It would just be a matter of time before the investigation turned in their favor.

# SIX

# CLOSING IN

*"These raids are only the beginning. We will hunt them all, and we will go into Brooklyn and any other borough to kick them out. The raids and seizures will continue until we break the back of the narcotics network."*
**Burton B. Roberts, Bronx U.S. Attorney**

ATTHEWS KNEW THAT law enforcement was on to him, but business was so good he made plans to move from his apartment in working-class Brooklyn to a mansion in upscale and affluent Todt Hill in the borough of Staten Island. The name Todt Hill comes from the old German word for "dead" and may refer to either a nearby cemetery or to the name some believed early Dutch settlers gave to the area because of the treeless, rocky exposures on the hilltops. Todt Hill is known for its panoramic views of New York harbor and for its elevation, which makes it the highest point on the Atlantic Coast from Miami to Florida. With seclusion, tranquility and lack of traffic, Todt Hill residents have long considered their neighborhood a virtual paradise compared to nearby New York City. Todt Hill residents—and in Matthews' time included such pillars of the community as borough president Robert Conner and assemblyman Lucio Russo—could afford to pay for this congenial environment. Even today that is true, for the yearly medium income of Todt Hill residents is nearly $150,000 and most houses sell for $1 million.

During the filming of *The Godfather* movie in 1972, an English Tudor House at 110 Longfellow Road in Todt Hill doubled as the Corleone compound. In 2011 the home, with eight bedrooms and a pub in its basement, sold for $2.9 million, according to published reports. It was only fitting that Todt Hill would be the scene for *The Godfather* movie. After all, over the years an assortment of Mob bosses from the Lucchese, Colombo and Gambino crime families have lived there.

This is why it seems strange that Frank Matthews would want to move his family to 7 Buttonwood Road in Todt Hill, given his volatile history with the Mob. "You'd think it would be the last place where Frank would want to live," explained Lew Rice, a retired DEA agent who investigated Matthews after his flight and disappearance. "No black people lived there, and some of the most powerful mobsters were just a stone's throw away from Matthews' house." In the Matthews era, the only blacks you could see in Todt Hill were the hired help: maids, chauffeurs, gardeners. Even today, blacks comprise just one percent of Todt Hill's population.

So why would Matthews want to move to such a place, far away from his homies, familiar haunts and exciting lifestyle? Maybe he just wanted to live in a neighborhood that fit the status and wealth of a drug kingpin. Or maybe he wanted to give his kids a better opportunity in life than he had. After all, Matthews did enroll them in the nearby exclusive Staten Island Academy where they would get an education that he could not even dream of as a kid. Roger Garay, a DEA retired agent who investigated Matthews, believes the move to Todt Hill was Barbara Hinton's idea. "She liked the finer things in life, and I think she wanted to move up the ladder and improve her status," Garay explained. "We know that Barbara was so proud of her new home that she reached out to a national magazine to see if it would do a feature story about the house. We learned Frank was not happy with that, even though, by moving to Todt Hill, he stuck out a like a sore thumb. He didn't want the publicity."

Matthews surely must have known who lived across the street from him a "stone's throw away": members of the Lucchese crime family and Paul Castellano, future godfather of the Gambino crime family. Tommy Lucchese (aka Three Finger Brown) lived on Buttonwood Road until his death on July 13, 1967. Born in Palermo, Sicily, in 1899, Lucchese rose to power on the New York Mob scene in the 1920s and became an ally of the powerful Boss of Bosses, Charles "Lucky" Luciano. Lucchese got his nickname, "Three Finger Brown," from the police, who, while booking him for stealing a car, noticed that he had only three fingers. Lucchese had lost a finger working in a factory when he was a kid. In 1953, after 22 years as an underboss, Lucchese became the boss of the Lucchese crime family and remained so until his death from a brain tumor and heart ailment. After Lucchese died, his family continued to live at their Todt Hill mansion.

Near the Luccheses lived Paul Castellano of the Gambino crime family, who, in the early 1970s, was fast becoming one of the family's most powerful bosses. Born in Brooklyn in 1915, Castellano, an eighth grade dropout, grew to be a giant of a man, 6' 2" and 270 pounds, and he used his size to intimidate fellow mobsters. Castellano's sister had married Carlo Gambino, his cousin and the future godfather of the crime family. "Big Paulie," as Castellano was called, was primed to move up the Mob ladder.

In 1966 Carlo Gambino appointed Castellano acting boss while he temporarily relocated to Florida to avoid pressure from law enforcement and the U.S. Naturalization and Immigration Service that wanted him deported back to Italy. Castellano had the authority to run the organization on a daily basis, yet Gambino remained the boss.

Castellano was as ruthless as he was powerful and not a godfather to mess with. He would be responsible for several murders, including that of his daughter's boyfriend, Vito Borelli, in 1975. Castellano heard that Borelli had likened his appearance to that of chicken magnate Frank Perdue who looked old and whom many people considered a buffoon.

Although from different crime families, the Luccheses and Castellanos had intermarried, and this allowed them to live amicably as neighbors. In 1962, Carlo Gambino's oldest son, Thomas Gambino, a capo in the Gambino crime family, married Tommy Lucchese's daughter Frances. Working as a powerful team, the two families controlled much of organized crime in New York City.

The Mob was not particularly enlightened on race relations, and it certainly did not like the idea of African Americans moving into their neighborhoods. "We know the Mob was really upset with Frank's presence in Todt Hill," said Gerard Miller, the BNDD agent who headed the Matthews' investigation. "We heard that the Mob sent a delegation to see Frank and tell him he was out of his league."

La Cosa Nostra, in fact, was so upset that Group 12 even started to receive "anonymous" intelligence from sources living across the street from the Matthews family. "They (the sources) were telling us about what was happening at Frank's place, who was coming and going, giving the license plate numbers," Bill Callahan explained. There were even rumors that Castellano planned to put a hit on Matthews. Jimmy Harris, a retired DEA agent who was the case agent for the Zach Robinson investigation, said that investigators learned from a wiretap that Castellano was planning to kill Matthews. "We don't know how Matthews responded, but we heard he took the threat seriously because he tried to arrange a meeting with Castellano," Harris said.

On the surface at least, Matthews did not seem bothered by the cold reception, and he went ahead with the construction of his new residence. He paid $23,000 for a vacant lot, and the mansion was estimated to have cost Black Caesar $200,000, a hefty price in 1971. No expense was too big for the wealthy drug lord, so he was an easy mark for dishonest contractors who ripped him off by overcharging for their work. One neighbor later said, "It's common knowledge he was really taken on the construction of his house. The contractors charged exorbitant prices."

Group 12 learned that all the work done on the mansion was paid for in cash. He paid the decorator $10,000, and the contractors, $250,000. One of the contractors was a specialist hired to install the marble floors, the gold plated fixtures and the swimming pool. Barbara Hinton's expensive tastes added to the bill. Mrs. Matthews did not like the way the kitchen was done originally, so she called in another contractor, telling him to rip everything out and do it all over again. "I don't care what it cost," Hinton reportedly told the contractor.

Once completed, though, the white two story house was magnificent: marble floors, gold fixtures, graceful columns supporting the roof, a hanging lantern worth $2,000, a swimming pool closed in by brick walls. Inside the mansion's large lobby a semicircular staircase spiraled to the second floor. The kitchen was state of the art, and the marble bathroom had gold faucets. Rumor had it that Black Caesar was planning to landscape the gardens for a golf course.

Keith Diamond, now a retired New York City public school teacher, had a chance to observe the opulent splendor of Todt Hill on a regular basis, working as a tutor for the Matthews' three children. Matthews hired Diamond in September 1971 when they were still living on Clarkson Avenue in Brooklyn, New York. Diamond also lived in Brooklyn, and after the move to Todt Hill, Diamond came to work five days a week, Monday through Friday. He was well paid for his tutoring services, about $125 per week, which Matthews handed to him in single dollar bills. In the early 1970s, Diamond was making $8,000 to $9,000 a year teaching, so the tutor's salary was excellent.

Diamond never did figure out the true occupation of his employer. Hinton volunteered once that she and her husband were in real estate, and Diamond accepted the explanation. "Frankly, I had a good thing going with the Matthews, so I didn't get curious or ask too many questions," Diamond explained. Nor did Diamond know anything about Matthews' neighbors in Todt Hill and was surprised to learn later that Matthews was living across the street from some of the La Cosa Nostra's most prominent crime families.

Diamond recalls Matthews as being "polite, nice and kind" and remembers the first time Black Caesar came to the door of his Clarkson apartment to let him in for a tutoring session. "He looked average, nothing out of the ordinary," Diamond recalled. "He had clothes laid out on the living room sofa: shoes, slacks, shirt, sweat jacket, hat. It looked as if Mrs. Matthews (Barbara Hinton) had Frank's finer threads out and was getting ready to go out on the town."

Diamond recalled Barbara Hinton as "young, in her 20s, thin, attractive, pleasant and well-spoken." As for the three kids, Sean, Andre and Frank Jr., their former tutor recalled that they were "well behaved," adding, "I was essentially helping them with their reports and homework. To be honest, they did not really need my tutoring." On one occasion, when Diamond came at Christmas to their Clarkson residence, the Matthews apartment looked like a toy store.

Diamond was really surprised the first time he saw the Todt Hill mansion. "The house was magnificent and a big change from Clarkson Avenue," he explained. "I saw something I never saw before or since. The sinks were handpainted. They were beautiful and tasteful."

Diamond experienced plenty of examples of Black Caesar's kindness and generosity. "One time, when living in Brooklyn, Matthews was going out of town to see a big fight and he asked me if I wanted to come with him," Diamond recalled. "When I was working for Matthews, I was 23 or 24 years old with a wife and three kids of my own. So I told him I couldn't get away right now. I had to work."

On another occasion, after tutoring the children, Diamond walked out of the mansion with Matthews to the circular driveway where a Cadillac Eldorado and two other luxury cars were parked. "I had just bought a '72 Chevy Malibu," Diamond recalled. "Matthews said to me, 'Oh, you bought a new car.' I said, 'Yes, I did.' He said that I could probably get $3,000 for it. I had paid $4,000. He told me that if I brought him $3,000 I could have any one of three cars for myself. I laughed and said, 'No thank you.' I was kind of embarrassed. I didn't know what to do. So, yes, he treated me well."

It appears the generous spirit ran deep in the Matthews household. Joan Diamond, Keith's wife, recalled how Barbara Hinton responded the day she learned Joan had just given birth to twins. "One afternoon, out of the blue, I got this phone call from Barbara Hinton. She said, 'Congratulations. It's great that you have twin sons. We have three sons ourselves.' She was complementing me… being very nice to me. About a week later after the call, I receive a package from Barbara. I opened it up and there are two quilt-like covers and covers for pillows. They were magnificent and beautiful. They were like something you'd buy in an expensive department store. I was taken aback. It was beautiful gift from someone who was basically a stranger to me."

As soon as the Matthews began moving into their new home, Group 12 continued its surveillance of Matthews' Todt Hill mansion. One night in late August 1972, Miller and Gray drove out to Buttonwood Road, got out of the car and circled around the house to the backyard. About 150 feet from the house, they started to crawl on their bellies along the field to get a closer look. Through binoculars, they peered into the house and could see that all was not peaceful inside. Matthews and John Darby seemed to be in a heated discussion and Hinton appeared to be pissed at their behavior. The agents could not hear anything, so they crawled a little closer to the house.

Miller and Garay thought they had the cover of darkness, but suddenly a light was switched on in the house, lighting up the backyard. The agents froze at the thought they might be spotted and that Matthews or perhaps Darby might even pull out a gun and shoot them. Garay reached for his gun, but the quick thinking Miller jumped on Garay and began simulating a gay lovers' embrace. Matthews spotted the couple. Garay glanced at the house out of the corner of his eye while Miller continued to straddle him. Garay saw Matthews poke Darby and mutter something to him. Darby laughed, then the light went out. Matthews had decided to let the two "lovers" have a little privacy. Garay and Miller stopped their simulated fornication. "I had to go along with it and make believe," Garay said with a laugh.

By the fall of 1972, after months of hard work, Group 12 was ready to move in on Matthews' organization. On September 15, 1972, the first two of Matthews' key lieutenants—John "Pop" Darby and Mickey Beckwith—were taken down. Agents raided Darby's Clarkson Avenue apartment and seized $145,480 in cash, a small quantity of narcotics, some weapons and various documents relating to drug deals and to expenditures made by the organization for mannite, baggies and other items. After the raid, the press wrongly described Darby as a minor figure in Matthews' organization. In reality, the bust was a major blow to Matthews' Philadelphia connection. Darby was arrested and later sentenced to prison on a state gun charge. Pop's wife, Thelma, assumed his role in Matthews' organization.

The same day, agents raided the OK Corral, Matthews' processing mill at 101 East 56$^{th}$ St., which Group 12 suspected was run by Mickey Beckwith. The OK Corral was the biggest heroin processing mill ever busted and gave the authorities a good idea about the size of Matthews' organization. Agents confiscated 2.5 million glassine envelopes stacked to the ceiling. With each of the glassine envelopes worth about $10 apiece after packing, the Matthews organization was getting ready to ship a mind-boggling $25 million worth of heroin. The bust showed that Black Caesar was like the Wal-Mart of the American drug trade. His ambition mandated that his organization controlled everything—cutting, packaging, distribution and sale.

Agents also confiscated drug-cutting paraphernalia: two 52-gallon mixing drums, together containing a half pound of unused heroin; a piece of paper that said, "Pop Smith (John Darby) $41,000"; weapons, including a machine gun and a collection of rifles for the processing mill crew to use to protect the narcotics mill from attack; and $148,480. As a bonus, the raiding party found a spiral bound notebook containing coded information about various drug deals. Interestingly, the mill included all the comforts of home—a sofa, armchair, a television set, stereo equipment and a bar stocked with some 50 bottles of liquor.

Based on the evidence gathered at the raid on the OK Corral, the U.S. government arrested and indicted Mickey Beckwith for "possession with intent to distribute a quantity of heroin and cocaine between 1968 and 1975." By this time, friction had set in between Matthews and Beckwith over a 40-foot yacht, the Double SS. Matthews had bought the boat, but Beckwith operated it. It was never taken out to sea but was used by Matthews and his crew to party. Matthews thought the boat would attract too much attention, and he wanted to get rid of it. Before that could happen, Uncle Sam seized the boat. Sure enough, ABC television filmed the surrender of the boat to the government at Governor's Island, and the story was broadcast all over the country.

At a meeting with John Darby on September 11, 1972, four days before the raids on the OK Corral and Darby's apartment, Matthews complained to Darby that Beckwith was becoming a problem because 'he didn't know who the boss was.'"

On October 31, 1975, Beckwith was convicted and sentenced to 12 years in jail, but authorities found Beckwith a tough felon to break. Beckwith adamantly told prosecutors he had no intention of snitching. Still, taking a key Matthews associate off the street was a big victory for Uncle Sam. "These raids are only the beginning," Burton B. Roberts, a Bronx U.S. Attorney, told the press. "We will hunt them all, and we will go into Brooklyn and any other borough to kick them out. The raids and seizures will continue until we break the back of the narcotics network."

The following day, Barbara Hinton and Thelma Darby talked twice on the telephone about the raids. Thelma told Barbara Hinton that she had to go to the Ponderosa (Matthews' other major heroin mill at 3D, 925 Prospect Place, Brooklyn), but she was glad she had not because she might have been arrested. The two women discussed the money ($148,480) that was seized at the OK Corral. Thelma also told Hinton that a woman had picked up a package of cocaine from John Darby at 130 Clarkson Avenue just prior to the agents' arrival and search of the apartment, and that only a small quantity of cocaine remained there. The information provided by the two women's loose lips formed the basis of a conspiracy charge when the government indictment came down in 1975.

In addition to these successes, another Matthews' associate went down. As explained earlier, the nature of Lou Cirillo's relationship with Frank Matthews is not known, and we will probably never know what it was, but the takedown of Lou Cirillo on October 12, 1972, was no doubt a blow to Black Caesar's organization. Cirillo was arrested in Miami wearing sunglasses, red and white stripped trousers, white shoes and a jersey wool shirt with vertical blue stripes.

In testimony before a U.S. Senate committee, Anthony Pohl, an official with the BNDD (Bureau of Narcotics and Dangerous Drugs), stated that during a period of seventeen months, from May 1970 to October 1971, Cirillo and his associates had smuggled in 1,500 kilos of heroin to the American market. With a kilo selling at the time for $10,500 a kilo, the heroin was worth $15,750,000 on the street.

Pohl and a team of BNDD agents went to Cirillo's modest home in the Bronx after being tipped off that Cirillo had a lot of money stashed there. The agents literally tore his house apart. In what looked like a sports room, agents found a tin box containing $100,000. They continued their search outside in the yard deep into the night. They then dug up the garden but found nothing until they dug in the ground under a window ledge. Bingo! They found a black plastic bag. Placed neatly in the bag were five packages, each containing $200,000. On May 25, 1973, Lou Cirillo was sentenced to 25 years in prison. Rumor had it that Cirillo sold Matthews his last kilo of heroin before Black Caesar jumped bail and disappeared.

Another kingpin went down on October 14, 1972, when agents raided a Schenectady Avenue address and confiscated books and records of Dutch Schultz (aka Ray Daniels), a big Matthews' customer, and arrested him. The records showed that Matthews was a major supplier of Daniels.

In June 1972 prosecutors convened a grand jury. The grand jury called more than 200 people, and according to estimates, 40 percent were convicted violators of the law. They were living in 10 states, as well as in the District of Colombia and three foreign countries (Haiti, France, and Venezuela) and a commonwealth of the U.S. (Puerto Rico). "All felonies must be presented to a grand jury as per the U.S. Constitution," Callahan explained. "In the Matthews case, the court convened a grand jury that lasted 36 months. We called numerous witnesses to help us weave our case." On November 21, 1972, Hinton appeared before the grand jury for the first time. Hinton provided some 20 pages of testimony, but then claimed "Privilege," or the right not to answer any more questions. The grand jury excused her.

Subsequently, the government sought an order granting Hinton immunity for her testimony. On February 16, 1973, Judge George Rosling of the U.S. District Court, Eastern District of New York, signed an order, authorizing the grand jury to recall Hinton for more testimony. But she still persisted in claiming her right not to testify and was shortly thereafter excused, apparently to enable the prosecutor and Hinton's lawyer time to discuss the immunity issue. In February and March 1973, Hinton was recalled two more times to testify, and she gave another 200 pages of testimony. Hinton was talking but not saying anything. After Hinton's testimony, prosecutors immediately began reviewing it for possible perjury prosecution. The court extended the grand jury until June 1974 so it could continue its investigation,

Numerous Matthews associates appeared before the grand jury. At this point they all invoked the 5th Amendment and refused to answer questions. Prior to his appearance, William Rosenbaum consulted with John and Martha Darby who advised him not to testify. Rosenbaum claimed his constitutional right not to testify when he appeared before the grand jury.

Group 12 had used several informants to try and move the investigation forward. Investigators, for instance, used a confidential informant (CI) to keep track of Matthews' movements. So when Matthews transferred his operation to a telephone with an answering service, they were immediately informed of this by the CI.

Much of the informants' information was either sketchy or worthless. Several Matthews associates—Beckwith and Darby, for example—had been tried or were awaiting sentencing, but they had not snitched. Still, the pressure of the investigation began to take its toll on the Matthews organization, and as the day of reckoning approached, the authorities were able to flip some of his associates.

One of the first to snitch was Babe Cameron. The homeboy from Durham, North Carolina had a problem with Matthews after one of Babe's customers overdosed from some heroin Matthews had sold him. Matthews had given Cameron the wrong instructions for cutting the heroin. Matthews apologized, but Cameron was charged with the murder of his customer. Although the charge was dropped, Cameron blamed Matthews for the mess.

Authorities turned to Norman Lee Coleman, a courier and small time dealer from Baltimore who had known Mathews since 1968. Coleman had worked a long time for Brother Carter and could tie him to Matthews from the early 1970s and to James Turk Scott, the prominent Baltimore Democrat and Matthews associate. Coleman brought Scott seven kilos of heroin from New York City. He kept one of the kilos for himself, but unfortunately for him, he also sold some of that dope to an undercover agent. Scott was arrested, but so was Coleman in March 1972. The thought of a long jail sentence of perhaps 30 years persuaded Coleman to cooperate, especially after the prosecutor assured Coleman he would not be prosecuted and offered him protection.

The authorities sent Coleman back on the streets as if it was business as usual and zeroed in on a big fish—Brother Carter, one of Matthews' biggest customers. When Coleman went to see Carter, he was wired with a transmitter whose range allowed the recording of conversations a mile away. Donald Keno James, Dutch Schultz's partner, also flipped when he sold dope to a BNDD undercover agent and faced three decades in jail. Neither Cameron, Coleman nor James were close to the Matthews organization, but they knew a lot about it. So their cooperation was a step forward in the investigation.

By December 1972, the Matthews investigation was on a roll. The wiretaps were making all kinds of connections. The raids on Darby's apartment and the OK Corral heroin processing mill provided evidence of a huge drug trafficking conspiracy. Informants were coming out of the woodwork. The surveillance may not have been successful, but Matthews was aware that the authorities were on to him, and this was beginning to put Black Caesar and his associates on edge and made them prone to mistakes.

A Group 12 report revealed that, by November 1972, the IRS had enough evidence to convict Matthews for tax violations committed in 1969 and 1970. Black Caesar could have received upwards of 14 years in prison, but the report also noted that Group 12 would continue its investigation before making a legal move on Matthews.

The authorities were about ready to swing the hammer and bring down an indictment in an attempt to destroy once and for all Black Caesar's drug trafficking empire.

Durham in the 1960s.

Frank Matthews .

Clarence Gardner, aka Reggie Collins, (center),
with friends at this 1971 birthday party.

Major Coxson of Baltimore worked with
Frank Matthews.

Fat Ty Palmer, associate of Frank Matthews.

Floyd Patterson, boxer, and his trainer, Buster Watson, a friend of Frank Matthews.

Al Bradley, co-director and co-producer, *The Frank Matthews Story* documentary.

Ike Atkinson, drug kingpin, supplied Matthews organization with heroin.

Matthews was a huge fan of Muhammed Ali.

Frank Matthews (right) with friends.

Lous Cirillo (worked with Frank Matthews).

Lew Rice—Retired DEA Special Agent who reopened the investigation of Matthews in Philadelphia and in New York City.

Las Vegas in the 1970s.

Dave O'Flaherty (left) and Mike Pizzi (right), U.S. deputy marshals who investigated Matthews.

Frank Matthews.

Nicky Barnes, (New York drug kingpin of the 1970s).

Jowalski at work with the NYPD.

Glenn Chism (left), Al Parrish, (right) at a hotel in Miami, Fla. regarding Frank Matthews investigation.

Bill Daley (as a youngster, Daley knew Matthews' children).

Courtney Brown, drug kingpin of the 1970s, met Matthews in Las Vegas.

Liddy Jones and a girlfriend.

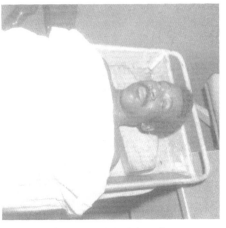

Matthews is escorted by officials following his arrest in Las Vegas.

Tommy Farrington, Pee Wee's homeboy, gets gunned down in Philadelphia.

William Callahan and the Deputy AG with the seized cash (about $1M) from one of the Matthews' seizures.

Bill Callahan (right), and Gerard Miller (left), in Caracas.

Ron Taylor, IRS agent.

William Callahan sitting at poolside in Caracas waiting for the Ok to interview Sereni.

Roger Garay investigated Frank Matthews.

Frank Matthews wanted poster.

Frank Matthews.

Tommy
Lucchese,
mobster.

Rick Talley, 1970s drug dealer who knew Matthews.

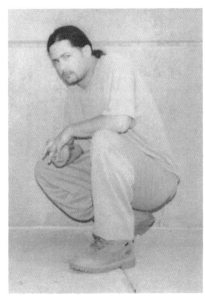

Seth Ferranti, Matthews biographer.

Debbie Nightwine, U.S. deputy marshal who investigated Black Caesar.

Paul Castellano, mobster.

Keith and Joan Diamond. Keith was the tutor for Frank Matthews' children.

Anthony "Ducks" Corallo, Mafioso of the powerful Lucchese crime family. Corallo was one of the investors in Matthews' C and I Carpet Service.

"Little" Melvin Williams (left) from HBO's The Wire, and Clinton "Shorty" Buise (right). Little Melvin was away in prison when Frank Matthews was the chief supplier of heroin in Baltimore. Buise met Matthews while gambling in New York City, and he would also see him in Baltimore from time to time.

# SEVEN

# BLACK CAESAR GOES DOWN

*".... I felt sick. I knew half of our indictment was just snatched away. Obviously something was going on in Caracas that we didn't know about."*
**William Callahan, Federal Prosecutor**

T
HE SEPTEMBER 15, 1972 raids by Group 12 on Pop Darby's apartment and the heroin processing mill at 101 East 56th St., the so called OK Corral, led to the seizure of a treasure trove of evidence and incriminating records, including narcotics, drug paraphernalia and money. More significant, however, was the major bust two weeks before of the Miami and Venezuelan-based narcotics trafficking networks that smuggled heroin and cocaine for Frank Matthews.

On August 30, 1972, Joseph Sereni arrived in Caracas, Venezuela, on Avianca Flight 71 from Paris, France, and entered the customs area of the international airport. Sereni, a courier for the Corsican Mafia, had a carry on overnight bag and two suitcases containing 58 pounds of heroin. The plan was for Evelio Mijares, an undercover Venezuelan police officer, whom the Corsican Mafia believed was a corrupt Venezuelan customs official, to pick up Sereni's two suitcases while Sereni went through customs. After clearing customs, Sereni left for his hotel without picking up his luggage. Meanwhile, Mijares took Sereni's two heroin-laden suitcases and went to the parking lot where he met Miguel Garcia (aka Marcelo Cabot) and Antonio Simon Orsatti-Serra, two Corsican Mafia members who had dealt drugs with Matthews. They all hopped into a car and went to the hotel where Sereni was staying and waited for them.

The group examined the stash, congratulated each other on their successful drug smuggling operation and left the hotel. Everybody was in a good mood, but that changed at about 11 p.m. that night when the Venezuelan police moved into action and arrested Sereni and his associates. The police seized the 25 hermetically sealed plastic bags containing the 58 pounds of heroin hidden in Sereni's luggage. In all, Venezuelan police arrested eleven suspects, including Rolando Gonzalez, Matthews' key drug connection in Venezuela.

In a coordinated raid in Miami, federal authorities arrested Orlando de la Madrid, a prominent Miami businessman, and Elpidio Hernandez, a drug dealer, seizing 12 pounds of heroin. The two were part of the Miami connection that supplied Matthews with cocaine. The heroin seized in the two busts had a street value of $126 million.

U.S. officials touted the busts as a model of international cooperation, even though Uncle Sam had long been concerned about corruption in Venezuela's government. "The arrests were an example of the coordination between the Venezuelan police and United States agents," John E. Ingersoll, Director of the BNDD (Bureau of Narcotics and Dangerous Drugs), boasted at the press conference announcing the big bust. Meanwhile, officials of Venezuelan's Judicial Police praised their brave undercover colleague, Evilio Mijares, for his successful portrayal of a corrupt customs official.

The drug game was over for the Corsicans in Venezuela when Group 12's wiretap on Matthews' Riverdale apartment revealed information about Caracas and the deal Sereni would arrange. Given the corruption in Venezuelan law enforcement, the BNDD's Caracas office monitored the arrests and made sure the 58 pounds of heroin did not disappear.

The press reported that Miguel Garcia was talking and had implicated Frank Matthews. Today, retired U.S. officials involved in the investigation neither confirm nor deny the press reports. As Callahan explained, "Unfortunately DEA and DOJ (Department of Justice) policy is that, if a CI (Confidential Informant) is not required to testify, his status may never be revealed. I was subject to those same regulations. The reason is that someone who is or was willing to testify is entitled to live the rest of his life worry free."

As the game was played, Garcia was wanted as a fugitive in the U.S., and he could have been sentenced to 12 years in prison for smuggling a load of 25 kilos on route to Frank Matthews. A 1976 U.S. Justice Department report revealed that all the defendants in the Venezuelan bust were actually released from prison.

It did not really matter because the Venezuelan authorities would not let Callahan and Miller interrogate Garcia or Orsetti. Sereni was a different story. In late September 1972, William Callahan, Group 12 supervisor Gerard Miller and Howie Schuman, a language translator, flew to Caracas to interview Sereni. William Callahan, a special attorney with the Office of Drug Abuse Law Enforcement (ODALE) who coordinated the federal government's investigation of Matthews, recalled the visit to the prison where Sereni was incarcerated: "The prison was located right in the middle of a barrio where chickens, goats and the wives and children of the prison officials all lived in ramshackle huts that were scattered about. There were no fences, but they had some of the buildings secured.

"First, we made an obligatory courtesy call for coffee with the warden and his staff in his ornate office. The warden rambled on and on, explaining to us the importance of guarding our credentials carefully. If a prisoner escapes with stolen badges, he warned, the person who lost the credentials had to serve the remainder of the fugitive's sentence. On the way to the warden's office, we saw big signs proclaiming this edict. So we hung on to our credentials as if it was a matter of life and death.

"Then a sergeant poked his head in the door and said the prisoner was ready to be interviewed. We all proceeded to a very bare room where a very pale and scared looking Sereni, probably in his mid-20's, was sitting, manacled to a table. He kept looking at us for help. In a corner of the room was a wheeled laundry cart with a mop handle lying in dirty water.

"Now, we had already drafted up the indictment that included the entire Caracas section of our case, including evidence against Sereni and one or two other drug dealers whom the local DEA had thrown in the mix. The warden made a big show of introducing us, and then left. A couple of fearsome looking guards stood by watching everything.

"We were feeling real good about the seizure and the arrest. My job now in the interrogation room was to ascertain Sereni's usefulness as a government witness at any forthcoming trial in New York City. We also knew that he had made admissions to the local police the night he was arrested, and I wanted copies of the transcripts to be translated. Miller started in with the questioning while Howie translated from the Spanish to Italian. Sereni only spoke Italian. Sereni assumed I was the highest ranking American official in the room and always looked directly at me with his answers. All I heard repeated was the refrain, "Agua, Agua", then a long rambling speech in Italian, which only Howie understood. I turned to Howie and said, 'I think he needs a glass or water. Get him some water.' Howie looked at me and said, 'Bill I need to talk to you and Jerry outside immediately.'

"So the three of us went out in the hall. "'Did you see the laundry cart sitting in the corner with the dirty water?' Howie asked. We learned that, on questioning Sereni the first night, they bent him over the edge of the cart and stuck his head under the dirty water for about ten long seconds. They yanked him up by his hair and told him he's now going under for 30 more seconds and then for a longer time until he drowns. Sereni caved and confessed. That was the "aqua" reference to the cart in the interrogation room.

"'There goes our entire Caracas case!' I told Howie and Jerry. They looked glum, but I had no choice. We couldn't use his confession in an American court because it was a forced confession. We had to decide if maybe we could get around it without using the confession at all.

A week later, Callahan and Miller were summoned to the Justice Department for a meeting with the assistant attorney general, the head of the Criminal Division. They were introduced to a lawyer from the CIA. Callahan recalled, "Without mincing his words, the CIA lawyer said, 'Gentlemen, we have decided it's best that you lop off your entire Caracas section of your indictment.' He wasn't requesting; he was ordering. I asked why and he said, 'because I said so.' He looked at us as if to say, 'Case closed!'

"The assistant attorney general then explained, 'You have some sharp lawyers up your way like that Gino Gallina guy who represents Matthews, and sharp lawyers are apt to put in an omnibus motion asking for any and all electronic surveillance anywhere in the world pertaining to his client's case. We don't like those types of motions. Get my drift?' We all slowly nodded. I felt sick. I knew half of our indictment was just snatched away. Obviously something was going on in Caracas that we didn't know about. So when we later indicted Matthews our case was based solely on the evidence we had on the domestic side. None of the defendants from the Venzuelan bust were any good to us because they had all been tortured. Sereni did his time. Then his Corsican cohorts paid a bribe and Sereni was released back to Italy. He's probably still alive somewhere."

The bust was a turning point for the Matthews investigation. "We knew we had to stop Matthews before he became too big," Callahan explained. "We now knew for sure that Matthews had an international connection. The DEA was able to marshal its forces pretty quickly and set the stage for arrest and seizure in Venezuela. We ended Matthews' direct international importation link, and we know no African American drug dealer would have that kind of connection again. It would have been beyond their skills and resources."

Matthews had also pissed off the Corsican gangsters with whom he was dealing in Venezuela. They had just lost a pile of money, and they undoubtedly viewed the disaster as Matthews' fault. He was careless on the phone, and it had cost them dearly. "The Corsicans had to dismantle their supply route to Miami, and they probably wanted to kill Matthews," Callahan said. "While we have no way of knowing what the CIA thought about the Venezuelan bust, they must have been furious with Matthews as well because the agency was very active in Venezuela. So in my view, the Venezuelan bust probably screwed up—or at least interfered with—their plans."

If Matthews knew that greed and carelessness had screwed up his international connection, he did not show it. He continued to operate with apparent carelessness—meeting drug connections in the street, talking in poorly disguised code on the phone and driving like a maniac. Was Black Caesar oblivious to what was happening around him, or was there method to his recklessness? Uncle Sam suspected that Black Caesar was stashing away millions. Even today, many of the officials who investigated Matthews believe he was preparing for his escape. But as pointed out earlier, money laundering tools were primitive in the Matthews era, so there is no way of knowing that for sure.

Investigators continued to close in on Matthews. In November 1972, BNDD agents had already arrested George Ramos, Miguel Garcia's godson and partner in crime who had provided Matthews with seemingly endless supplies of cocaine. "It was quite unusual for a black guy to come down to Miami and buy coke from the Cubans," recalled Jack Lloyd, a retired DEA agent who investigated George Ramos and the Matthews-Miami drug connection. "Matthews would come down to Miami with $100,000 or more and buy narcotics." When Ramos was arrested, Lloyd personally brought him to New York for interrogation.

Ramos was personable, smart, good-looking and younger than Matthews. He quickly sized up his options and knew what he had to do. "When they brought Ramos to New York for questioning, he flipped right away," Garay revealed. "We interrogated him for several days about Matthews and his organization. He told us about how Matthews had worked to establish the Venezuelan connection. We knew Ramos would be an important witness against Matthews when we were ready to indict him."

On November 22, Ramos appeared before the grand jury and testified against Matthews. Ramos testified about various major deliveries of narcotics involving Frank Matthews and his organization between April and September 1972. Ramos recalled one meeting in June 1972 when Matthews fronted $100,000 to Ramos and Garcia for a future shipment of 100 kilos of heroin.

Marshals guarded Ramos around the clock while they made arrangements for his entry into the Federal Witness Protection Program. Once that was done, the Marshals moved Ramos to Portland, Oregon, for safe-keeping while they finished their takedown of Black Caesar.

After a year of investigation, the authorities were ready to put the cuffs on Black Caesar. On December 20, 1972, prosecutors obtained a warrant for Matthews' arrest, but it was the holiday season, and authorities felt no urgency to execute the warrant. Matthews was able to spend a quiet Christmas with his family. Then, on New Year's Eve 1972, investigators got wind that Matthews, his girlfriend Cheryl Denise Brown, and several suitcases had left town for Las Vegas. He spent about a week in Las Vegas before traveling to Los Angeles and the Super Bowl game between the Miami Dolphins and Washington Redskins. Group 12 alerted the Las Vegas BNDD office and gave instructions to keep Matthews under surveillance, and agents tailed Black Caesar, but he still liked to have fun with his pursuers. Agents lost him several times in traffic. Worried that Matthews might be planning to disappear, Group 12 ordered the BNDD's Las Vegas office to arrest him.

At 11 a.m., January 5, 1973, Matthews and Brown were picked up at Las Vegas' McCarran International Airport as they were about to board a plane for Los Angeles. Matthews offered no resistance. One hour later, he was arraigned in court before U.S. Magistrate Joe Ward. He had $5,000 on him and tried to give it to Brown so she could have money to get back home. The Marshals took Brown into custody, even though there was no warrant for her arrest. They searched through Brown's purse and found a motel key. They charged her with possession of burglary tools. The authorities told the press that the charge was a technical complaint pending further investigation.

The federal warrant charged Matthews with possession and intent to sell 18.6 kilos (almost 41 pounds) of cocaine between April and September of 1972. The street value of the cocaine was estimated to be worth between $1 million and $4.5 million. The federal warrant named George Ramos as the man who told federal investigators that he and Matthews had flown to Miami and delivered large sums of money to Miguel Garcia in return for cocaine.

Excited by the news of Matthews' arrest, Bill Callahan and Gerard Miller caught the first plane to Las Vegas. The next day they were in the courtroom for a bail bond hearing for Matthews before magistrate Joseph L. Ward. Black Caesar was as cocky as ever. "We were literally face to face," Callahan recalled. "He told us that we had nothing on him and that he would be out in no time."

Prosecutors argued before the magistrate that a high bail was necessary to insure Matthews remained in jail until he could be extradited to New York. They contended that Black Caesar was a threat to flee and had the money to do it. To make their point, they explained that as a big gambler, he had lost up to $120,000 in the casinos. They claimed he had millions of dollars stashed away in safety deposit boxes in Las Vegas.

None of the authorities, however, expected Ward's decision. He set bail at $5 million, the highest bail in U.S. history. As Matthews left the Las Vegas courtroom, stunned and handcuffed to a federal marshal, a small, bald, bespectacled nondescript looking man walked up to him and identified himself as an IRS agent. He pulled out a piece of paper from his briefcase and handed it to Matthews.

"What's this?" Matthews asked.

"It's a termination assessment," the IRS agent replied, explaining in precise detail, "Your taxable income for the year just ending December 31, 1971, was approximately $100 million. You owe $7,007,165 in taxes, plus a $6 lien fee." The IRS's tax estimate was based on evidence of alleged criminal activities and was used in cases where the IRS feared that collecting the money might be a problem.

An incredulous Mathews looked at the IRS agent and said, "How the fuck am I supposed to pay that?"

The IRS agent did not miss a beat, "Preferably in cash."

The assessment put Matthews in a bind. To get his client's bail reduced Stanley Kaufman, Matthews' lawyer who had flown in to Las Vegas from New York, had told Magistrate Ward that his declared income for 1971 was just $200,000. Matthews, however, would have to pay the $2.5 million bond plus the $7,009,165 that he owed to the IRS if he hoped to make bail. But he faced tax evasion charges if he paid that amount. After all, how does a man with a declared income of $200,000 get that kind of money?

The enormous size of the bail caught the press's attention, and overnight Matthews went from being an unknown drug dealer to a media curiosity, especially when authorities began describing Matthews as the "biggest narcotics man" in New York City. New York newspaper article headlines described Black Caesar as "the mystery man of Todt Hill" and revealed how life had been "high style for (the) dope suspect."

A Matthews neighbor told the *New York Daily News,* "Matthews is a curiosity in the neighborhood because he's the only black here. He's lived here a year or two. It's no surprise to hear about his arrest. When I told some people recently that I lived on Buttonwood Road, they said, 'Oh, you're right near the Harlem dope king.'"

Another neighbor described Matthews as being protective of his privacy, although he appeared to be a lavish spender. "I've never seen him except when he drove by in one of his cars. He has about $10,000 worth of cars, including a Rolls Royce parked in his driveway. It's common knowledge he was taken to the cleaners on his home, charged exorbitant prices by the contractors."

Eventually, Keith Diamond, the Matthews tutor, read press reports about how the police had put Matthews' house under surveillance. At first the reports brought a chill to his spine. Then he smiled. Diamond remembered how he would show up at Matthews' Todt Hill mansion carrying a briefcase and looking like a Matthews associate. The authorities never brought him in for questioning.

"It was all over the news…the arrest in Las Vegas of the big New York drug dealer," he recalled. "Then I started to get phone calls about the arrest from my parents in Florida, from my friends… Did you hear? Did you hear? It was him, Frank Matthews. Eventually, I was disappointed because I needed the job."

With bail set, the authorities were ready to transport Matthews back to New York City. The U.S. Attorney's office prepared an extradition request, while Callahan and Miller met with IRS agents assigned to the case under the IRS's Narcotics Trafficking Program. The judge set a bail hearing for January 7, but Stanley Kaufman told the judge his client was ready to return voluntarily to the Eastern District of New York and asked that his bail be reduced to $500,000. The government strenuously objected to any reduction in bail. In an effort to be fair, Magistrate Ward reduced Matthews bail in half to $2.5 million. "We weren't too happy about the bail reduction, but we knew Matthews was going back to New York City in chains," Callahan explained.

At the time of Matthews' arrest, drug kingpins Courtney Brown and Eddie Jackson were also locked up in Clark County jail with Matthews as a part of a federal roundup in Las Vegas. "I said to Matthews, 'Got you, too, homie?'" Brown said. "Frank laughed and said, 'Yeah, man. We all hot. Those motherfuckers! I don't care what they got. I'm going to get my bond posted, and then I'm gone.'"

Callahan was eager to interview Matthews while he was still in Las Vegas' Clark County Jail. "When we went to see Matthews, he stonewalled us completely," Callahan recalled. "He said he didn't want to speak with white agents or prosecutors. So we called Marshal Butler, the U.S. Marshal in Brooklyn, who was black, and asked him to come out to Las Vegas to interrogate Matthews. Butler spoke to Matthews alone. Matthews opened up and told Butler he was tired of paying huge amounts of money to La Cosa Nostra and to a group of Jewish businessmen in Brooklyn that was distributing heroin. We never did figure out who those Jewish businessmen were, but we did learn that Matthews was buying heroin from the Mob and they were overcharging him. Matthews hated the Italians (mobsters) because they hated the blacks."

On January 13, federal marshals escorted Matthews to New York City. The authorities let Brown go, but it is unclear how she returned home. According to Donald Goddard's account in *Easy Money*, the ever faithful Hinton left her children with her mother and fled to Las Vegas to be with Matthews. Then Brown, Hinton and Matthews all flew back to New York on a government plane, but Brown and Hinton did not say anything to each other. The problem with this account is that officials who were on the plane with Matthews don't recall Hinton being in Las Vegas at the time. "Donald Goddard's facts were sometimes off a bit," Callahan said.

On the plane, Matthews hinted that he might be willing to make a deal. Callahan told Matthews the best he could do was a ten-year sentence. The other law enforcement officials on the plane expressed agreement. Matthews ended the "negotiations" abruptly, snapping: "Forget it. I'll do the time."

Matthews was taken to the West Street Detention Center where he remained while prosecutors filed a series of indictments against him, including tax evasion and conspiracy to distribute cocaine in the Eastern District of New York. Several superseding indictments followed. The Matthews case was getting increasingly complicated, and the prosecution wondered if they would be able to go to trial soon.

Matthews decided to replace Stanley Kaufman with prominent criminal defense attorney Gino Gallina whose law firm was noted for handling tough cases. The handsome Bronx native Gallina was a New York Assistant District Attorney from 1965 to 1969 before leaving to defend some of the most notorious gangsters of the Matthews era, including Frank Lucas of *American Gangster* movie fame and Francois Chiappe, a Corsican charged with running a narcotics ring that spanned three continents and smuggled six tons of heroin into the U.S.

Gallina was a magnet for controversy, and while acknowledged in the legal community as a brilliant defense criminal lawyer, he was also viewed as shady and corrupt. "His (Gallina) problem was that he could never tell the white hats from the black hats," one chief of detectives with organized crime task force told the press, "He liked the wiseguy lifestyle...the flashy goals, the women."

Gallina was suspected of passing confidential court information to his gangster clients. Several witnesses were subsequently murdered, but the complicity of Gallina was never proven. Two years after representing Matthews, Gallina was implicated in an international heroin trafficking ring and named a co-conspirator in a federal trial, along with several organized crime figures, although he was never indicted. Gallina eventually became a key witness before a Newark grand jury investigating Genovese crime family members, including Vincent "The Chin" Gigante who would become boss of the family in 1981. The press later dubbed the mobster "The Oddfather" and "The Enigma in the Bathrobe" because he often wandered the streets of Greenwich Village in his bathrobe and slippers, mumbling incoherently to himself. Gigante would eventually admit that it was all an elaborate act to avoid prosecution.

Matthews remained in the West Street Detention Center for two months. Warren Robinson, a former drug dealer from Washington, D.C. who would soon spend 35 consecutive years in prison, was incarcerated at the detention center when Matthews was brought there in January 1973. "Heavies like Matthews don't talk openly in jail with anybody about their cases or their plans," Robinson said. "But by now, everybody in West Street had heard of Frank. I remember how some Italian mobsters (incarcerated at the detention center) were tapped out and Frank gave them some money. He had so much money it didn't mean anything to him."

Matthews tried to keep a low profile at the detention center, but an incident that happened when Matthews' lawyer Gino Gallina came to see him, had tongues wagging. "Most everybody knew about Gino Gallina," Robinson recalled. "He would come by and meet with Matthews in the lawyer's lounge. Gallina would bring papers for Frank to sign. But then one day, Gallina came by and said to Frank, 'You trying to play some kind of joke on me?' Frank said, 'What?' Gallina told Frank, 'There's nothing in the vault.' Frank exploded, grabbed Gallina and threw him to the ground. The guards rushed over and restrained Frank. 'You motherfucka!' Frank yelled. 'You never gonna spend that money.' The guards hauled Frank away. The word went around that Gallina had ripped Frank off for something like a million dollars. Gallina was crazy. He didn't know how dangerous Frank could be."

Rumors abounded that the money of other gangsters, whom Gallina represented, had also disappeared. So Gallina had no shortage of dangerous enemies. He managed to survive another three years pissing off his underworld clients. One of them was Frank Lucas who once accused Gallina of being involved in the disappearance of $3 million Lucas claimed he had stashed in a Lucas deposit box. "On March 5, 1977, Gallina came to see Lucas at Riker's where he was incarcerated," recalled Lew Rice, a retired DEA agent, who is familiar with the Matthews and Lucas investigations. "Lucas demanded, 'Where is money!' Then he jumped across the table and attacked Gallina."

A few hours later, Gallina was in the company of a lady and dining at a restaurant in the vicinity of Carmine and Varick Streets in Manhattan. As Gallina stepped from the car, a lone gunman walked up and shot him eight times. An ambulance rushed to the scene, but it was too late. Gallina lay sprawled on the street, dead.

Matthews and/or his associates were suspected of doing the hit. "We interviewed Gallina's law partner and learned that Matthews had used their firm to hold cash in escrow, but it had disappeared," Callahan said. This is, however, mere speculation. Matthews was part of a long line of disgruntled clients, any of whom could have put the hit on Gallina. Besides, why seek revenge three years after the dastardly act?

Authorities suspected Matthews of conducting his business as usual behind bars. He conferred with John Darby almost daily, and authorities received information that Matthews had made arrangements for his organization's management while he remained in prison. Donald Conner was now supposedly the acting kingpin, but many sources doubt he had what it took to be an interim kingpin.

On April 9, 1973, three months after his incarceration at the West Street Detention Center, Matthews appeared in court before Judge Anthony J. Travia for a bail reduction hearing. The prosecutors' worst fears came about. Judge Travia reduced Matthews' bond to $325,000 and ordered him to report to the U.S. Attorney's office and stay within the jurisdiction of the Eastern District. Incredibly, Matthews' associates had already anticipated the bombshell decision. On April 2, seven days before the bond hearing, Matthews' Aunt Marzella had called a meeting in Durham of Matthews supporters: Georgia Surety, the Atlanta bond firm;

and Edward L. Stanton, the representative of the insurance company underwriting the bond.

The Matthews delegation offered real estate property as collateral for the bond, but Stanton told the supporters that the value of the real estate did not meet the bond and that he needed at least $100,000. Marzella made a phone call, and a little later, Stanton himself received one call. Stanton then met with a young woman in the parking lot of the First Union Bank. She handed him a plastic bag wrapped in Christmas paper. Stanton took the money to the bank and counted it in private. The plastic bag contained $100,000.

With the bond money raised, a cocky Matthews strutted out of court to freedom. Prosecutors were outraged at Judge Travia's decision. Investigators suspected a payoff or two may have been made. "We did discuss the word 'corruption' internally, of course, especially since Gallina was involved, and he had access to a lot of cash," Callahan recalled. "But eventually the concern petered out. We were more focused on getting Matthews than having to deal with the stupidity of one judge."

Matthews was free, but he no longer had his Todt Hill mansion. The IRS had seized the property, and Barbara Hinton and their three kids now lived in an apartment at 2785 Ocean Parkway in Brooklyn. Donald Conner was living there as well, but Matthews was once again in charge of his organization. By late June 1973, Group 12 received information that Matthews had squirreled away perhaps as much as $20 million, but they could not verify it.

Matthews was spotted in meetings with known narcotics dealers, and investigators received word he was still distributing narcotics. "We couldn't keep tabs on Matthews," Garay said. "We were stretched thin and simply didn't have the manpower to watch him 24-7. All we could do was hope and pray he would keep showing up in court."

# EIGHT

# FLIGHT

*"We (in Durham) heard that Frank came through Durham after he fled New York with suitcases full of money."*
**Ricky Johnson, Durham native**

B Y THE SUMMER OF 1973, Matthews had more than law enforcement and indictments to contend with if he stuck around for the inevitable trial. He could see the drug scene in America and his own personal situation changing. It would be a struggle—if not a battle—to hold onto his criminal empire. Matthews knew informants were stepping forward, and who knew what they would squeal about him and his organization once they began facing the prospect of long prison sentences. Mickey Beckwith was a case in point. Matthews' relationship with Beckwith had cooled, and he had to worry about what would come out in Beckwith's trial, scheduled to begin before Matthews' trial.

Norm Coleman had flipped, as had George Ramos. Matthews knew Ramos would reveal all about the Cuban drug connection in Miami. Ramos had worked out a deal with Uncle Sam that put him in the Federal Witness Protection Program. Three days after Matthews jumped bail, federal marshals took George Ramos to Portland, Oregon, after sentencing before Judge Charles B. Fulton in Miami. Ramos had pled guilty to one charge of drug conspiracy and was sentenced to four years imprisonment. With credit for time served, Ramos spent 20 months in jail. He would be the star witness in the 1975 trial in New York City of 18 Matthews associates.

Matthews also had to deal with the increasingly unstable illicit drug market. Shortages of heroin were becoming increasingly prevalent as law enforcement continued its relentless assault on the French Connection, still the major supplier of the drug. With the heroin supply tight and expensive, a kilo could sell for as much as $200,000, ten times the normal price.

It was tough enough for Matthews to find the heroin and cocaine to keep his narcotics empire afloat, but he also had to deal with the chronic shortages of quinine and mannite, the cutting or filler materials used in the packaging of heroin. By the summer of 1972, Matthews had many kilos of heroin in stock he could not sell because he lacked cutting materials. If that 100 kilo shipment of heroin from Venezuela had gone through, Matthews would have needed more than ten times the amount of cutting materials to cut the heroin at five percent strength of purity.

Matthews ordered Pop Darby, his chief lieutenant in Philadelphia, to find a solution for his cutting materials problem. For help, Darby turned to Walter Rosenbaum, a bail bondsman, businessman and old friend whom he had known for 25 years. Rosenbaum knew what a mannite or quinine shipment would be used for, but, initially, he had no problem with it. He checked with several American pharmaceutical companies but had no success in finding a supplier. Knowing mannite was an Italian product, he contacted the Italian consulate in New York City and obtained a list of manufacturers in Italy. Rosenbaum wrote the companies, asking them prices and delivery dates.

Initially, Rosenbaum worked out a deal for a trial shipment from Santana Progal of Genoa, Italy, to deliver 252 tons of mannite to Darby upon payment of a certified check for $1,814.409. It looked as if Rosenbaum had solved Matthews' cutting materials problem, but then he had second thoughts. What if the trial shipment was successful, and Darby wanted more and more filler? Rosenbaum did not like the answer, concluding that something would eventually go wrong. Time in the slammer for him would be the inevitable result.

So Rosenbaum called the Philadelphia office of the BNDD (The Bureau of Narcotics and Dangerous Drugs) and revealed the scheme to the authorities. In June 1973, just prior to Matthews jumping bail, Rosenbaum agreed to snitch on the Frank Matthews organization for Uncle Sam.

Meanwhile, Philadelphia, Matthews' biggest market, was becoming so unstable because of his problems with the Black Mafia that Matthews decided to move Pop Darby to New York City and the safety of his Brooklyn apartment building. In March 1971, the Black Mafia had murdered Fat Ty Palmer, Matthews' close associate and biggest Philly distributor, in front of 800 shocked people in the popular Club Harlem in Atlantic City. By the time Matthews was about to jump bail, the Black Mafia had grown substantially in power, and in the coming months, other Matthews associates would go down violently as well.

Interestingly, some law enforcement officials who investigated the Matthews organization believed that Matthews was responsible for the murder of the drug dealing politician Turk Scott in Baltimore. However, the killer was actually Sherman Dobson, the son of prominent Baltimore minister, who said he committed the murder on behalf of Black October, a shadowy black Muslim group that wanted to rid the Baltimore streets of drugs.

The Black Mafia was not the only group challenging Matthews for control of turf. Vigilantes, including Black Panthers, Black Muslims and some Rastafarians, had implemented a policy in black neighborhoods demanding drug pushers be shot on the spot. "The self-righteous vigilantes were frustrated by the lack of law enforcement activity in their communities and by the corruption of the police and had no other motive but to clean up their neighborhoods," explained Robert J. Kelley, an expert on U.S. organized crime.

The vigilantes included the not-so-righteous Black Muslim commando groups that were seeking to collect 10 percent kickbacks on each drug deal consummated in their neighborhood. But Matthews was not the type to be intimidated. He bought a shipment of automatic weapons and sent his men out to Harlem and other black neighborhoods in New York looking for the commandos. War broke out. Black Caesar held his own but realized this was not the kind of environment in which to conduct business.

On July 2, 1973, Matthews failed to appear in Brooklyn federal court to plead to a new indictment superseding one of the six indictments that the court had already handed down. The next day, he was declared a fugitive from justice.

Black Caesar's last days in the Big Apple and his departure have become the stuff of legend. Today, stories—wild stories—abound about Matthews' last days of freedom. They recall how he gave away money, bushels of it, in fact. Some sources say he did say goodbye to some of his good friends and spread some of his wealth around. One old timer from the Matthews era told writer Seth Ferranti, "We heard Frank left New York with 55 gallon drums filled with money." Durham native Ricky Johnson revealed, "We (in Durham) heard that Frank came through Durham after he fled New York with suitcases full of money."

Reggie Collins (aka Clarence Gardner), a drug dealer from the Matthews era and currently an inmate at Baldwin State Prison in Hardwick, Georgia, said he was one of the last of Matthews' friends to see him before he disappeared. "It was 4 am. and we were at Flaps on 119th St. (in New York City)," Collins recalled. "Frank said he was heading out of town and not coming back. I watched him drive off in a 1972 Ford Thunderbird, black body, white top. Never saw him again." Collins did not recall Black Caesar giving out money at the club like it was candy.

Homeboy Gattis Hinton and mistress Cheryl Denise Brown also disappeared at about the same time as Matthews. Gattis Hinton also faced charges, but investigators dismissed the idea that he went on the run with Black Caesar. Cheryl Denise Brown, however, was seen frequently with Mathews when he was free on bail, and investigators believed she left with him. A material witness warrant was issued for Brown, meaning that the authorities did not want to arrest her for a crime, but they did want to question her.

Investigators believe that Matthews had laundered perhaps as much as $20 million in preparation for his flight and that he had most likely left the country. But just a month later, after Matthews' disappearance, Michael Bramble, a NYPD detective, claimed to have spotted him behind the wheel of a white Cadillac convertible. According to Bramble's report, he chased Matthews but could not call for help because his car had no radio. When Bramble tried to cut in front of the Cadillac, Matthews ran him off the road. The Cadillac was later found abandoned with blood stains on the backseat. The blood turned out not to be human.

Would Matthews still be in New York City a month after jumping bond? "We had to believed Detective Bramble because he was a police officer in good standing," said Bill Callahan. In any case, police and federal agents began thinking that maybe Matthews did not flee the country, so the focus of their manhunt shifted back to the U.S.

When questioned by Group 12 investigators, Donald Conner claimed he drove Matthews to the airport. "Conner told us Frank and Cheryl left for Houston by air," revealed Group 12 detective Roger Garay. "We checked the flights for both of them using their real names. No luck. Maybe he had a new identity or worse yet, a fake passport made." More than 15 years later, Conner would tell U.S, Marshals that he gave Matthews his draft card to use as identification. If Cheryl Denise Brown did indeed board the plane with Matthews, what did she use for identification?

On January 25, 1974, the newly created Drug Enforcement Administration (DEA), the successor to the BNDD (Bureau of Narcotics and Dangerous Drugs), announced an award of $20,000 leading to the arrest of Frank Matthews. It was the biggest reward since the one offered in 1931 for John Dillinger, the famous bank robber of the Depression era. The authorities were confident the reward would result in good leads to Matthews' whereabouts.

After NYPD detective Michael Bramble claimed to have chased Matthews in New York City a month after he jumped bail, the manhunt turned its focus to the domestic scene. The authorities circulated thousands of wanted posters throughout the country and law enforcement received numerous calls from people, claiming to have seen the fugitive. The authorities thought they had Matthews when one tip led to Syracuse, New York, and a downtown rooming house. Hundreds of local police, state police and federal agents sealed off the area around the house, only to find when they moved in that the suspect with the name of Frank Matthews was more than 80 years old.

When Group 12 alerted federal law enforcement agencies in North Carolina that Matthews was a fugitive, the hunt for Matthews got more complicated. Detective Bramble had Black Caesar in New York a month after he jumped bail. Conner had him on a plane to Houston, date unknown. Now Ron Taylor, the IRS agent who had investigated possible money laundering links between Matthews and Marzella Steele Webb, received a tip that Black Caesar was in Durham at the First Union National Bank. "Another agent and I rushed to the bank," Taylor recalled. "I asked the bank manager if he had seen Matthews. He said, 'Oh, you just missed him.' He nodded to the back door and said, 'He went that way.' I ran out the back door to the parking lot and saw a car speed away. It could have been a Lincoln; I can't say for sure. But I remember that the car fit the description of a car Matthews owned. He had to be in the car, but I couldn't really see who was in it. That's how close we came to catching Frank Matthews. We missed him by minutes. I could have been a hero!"

Wherever Black Caesar had gone, Group 12 believed he had brought a lot of money with him and that development could spell trouble for the investigation. Rich Broughton, an agent in the BNDD's Greensboro, North Carolina office got a call from Gerry Miller, Group 12 supervisor and head of the Matthews investigation in New York City. "Miller asked if we could send somebody to Durham to look for Matthews," Broughton recalled. "Miller had an arrest warrant for Matthews. He told me, 'Don't arrest him. Just detain him. We will come down from New York City and lock him up.' I said: 'Why shouldn't we arrest him? If we find Matthews, you can bet we are going to lock his ass up.' Miller said, 'We heard Matthews fled New York with $2 million. He has enough money to bribe anybody he comes into contact with. Just stand by. We got a team here in New York. We will come down and arrest him.'"

Broughton continued: "Can you believe that? If we caught Matthews, all he had to do was flash some money and we would let him go. That was the biggest insult you can give a fellow agent. Miller was telling me that he didn't trust us. I told Miller, 'I'm not going to Durham!' I called the Durham police and told them, 'If you catch Matthews, lock him up and don't bother to call the BNDD.'"

In jumping bail, Matthews left the people who had put up the money holding the bag, so to speak. To meet the $325,000 bond, a delegation of friends and family members led by Matthews' Aunt Marzella had raised $100,000 and posted some of Matthews' properties in New York City as collateral. On July 20, 1971, Federal judge Anthony J. Travia ordered the forfeiture of $325,000 bail that Matthews posted.

The bonding company, Public Service Mutual Inc. did not appear in court to protest the forfeiture. The press noted that the biggest signer of the bond was Julius Sterling Sales of Durham, who put up his business Jake's Garage, estimated to be worth $100,000. To collect, the bonding company would have to obtain a foreclosure.

In early July 1973, Barbara Hinton met with Edward Stanton, the representative of the insurance company that had posted Matthews' bond. Hinton told Stanton that there would be no need for his company to proceed legally against the properties her common-law husband had posted as collateral. If Frank is alive, he will re-pay your insurance company, Hinton assured Stanton. Sure enough, on July 19, 1973, two men delivered $225,100 in cash to Stanton's insurance company. The bond was repaid.

The insurance company was not the only entity to which Black Caesar owed money. The IRS was relentlessly pursuing the $7,009,165 in back taxes that Matthews owed the U.S. government. To recover some of the debt, the IRS auctioned Matthews' Todt Hill mansion and its contents in mid-January 1974. The auctioneer was IRS agent Vincent DiPaolo, who oversaw an eight man staff that ran the liquidation sale for the IRS's Manhattan office at 120 Church Street.

Undeterred by the abominable weather and the hazardous driving conditions, nearly a hundred prospective buyers, many of them requesting anonymity, crowded into the living room of the Matthews house at 7 Buttonwood Road. Nobody from the Matthews family attended the auction. "The auction realized just about what it should have," said Claire Brown, a Staten Island auctioneer, who appraised the furnishings. That was Brown's delicate way of saying that the IRS had to settle for a "pauper's portion" of the true value of the contents it sold.

For a mere $5,085, eleven people walked off with an assortment of furnishings, including everything from a commode chair to a 15-foot marble top end table valued at $400. A hefty young woman in skintight pants and an expensive looking fur coat took home a huge credenza from the living room for $330. She declined to give her name to the press because she had called in sick to her boss in order to attend the auction. The single biggest chunk of cash, $1,500, was paid for the furnishings in the master bedroom: a mirror, night table, king-size bed, color TV with remote control, and a shoe chest with 25 compartments. The lowest bid of the evening was $55 for a collection of Christmas decorations, toys and a hobby horse.

Earlier, the IRS had tried to auction off the house, but the court gave priority to the lending institution for the mortgage. The Matthews house, valued at $250,000, sold for $128,000 at auction to Mrs. Ann Mae Cotogna of 925 Todt Hill Road. Paul Cotogna, Mrs. Cotogna's husband, attended the auction, and he told the press that his wife's purchase was a "business decision," meaning the property could be re-sold.

After the IRS seized the Todt Hill property, Hinton and her three children moved to 3333 Henry Hudson Parkway. Eventually, the Matthews family settled into a house on 95th Street between Ditmas and Avenue B in a middle-class Brooklyn neighborhood. Bill Daley and Dexter Lezama, two kids not yet in their teens, befriended the Matthews children. Daley and Lezama, now in their 40s, remember Hinton and her children as "unpretentious, nice people" who "obviously had money but never flaunted it." "Mrs. Hinton was beautiful and down-to-earth, and you would never know that she and the children were connected to Frank Matthews," Lezama explained. "They were good neighbors." Hinton owned a grocery store in the neighborhood."

Of the three Matthews brothers, Daley and Lezama were the closest to Sean (nicknamed Man) because they were about the same age. "Sean never talked about his father," Daley explained. "I can only recall one time when the subject of our fathers came up. He asked me what my father did for a living. I explained that he was a police officer back in Jamaica. I asked him what his father did. Sean hesitated and then said, 'My father is a gangster.' I just looked at him and laughed, thinking he was joking. But now I know he was serious."

The Hinton home was nicely furnished, but both Daley and Lezama thought it odd that it did not contain any photos of the father. "We never saw anything in the house that indicated who their father was," Daley recalled. "Come to think of it, they never talked about him."

Eventually, the Matthews, Daley and Lezama families all moved out of the neighborhood, and they lost touch. "I heard through the grapevine that Sean later got into trouble with dogs... dog fighting, I think," Lezama said. "He had a Doberman when he was living in our neighborhood. I would love to see him again. He was a good guy."

While federal and state authorities conducted a massive manhunt for Frank Matthews, his criminal organization struggled to survive without their kingpin. The competitors moved in and bodies began dropping in New York City. Two weeks after Matthews skipped town, 33-year old William Perry and his bodyguard, 40-year old Lloyd Clemmons, were machine gunned to death in Perry's Bronx apartment. Perry, who was believed to be a Matthews business associate, was co-owner of the Club Barron, a popular Harlem jazz bar.

The authorities speculated the double hit was the start of a gang war for Matthews' drug empire. Their speculation seemed to be confirmed when the bodies of other drug dealers started to litter the streets of Harlem, Bedford Stuyvesant and the South Bronx.

Group 12 continued its surveillance and efforts to collect evidence that could help them take down the organization. On several occasions, investigators spotted Matthews associates making drug buys. On December 5, 1973, in Philadelphia, for instance, agents tailed John Darby and an associate to a gas station where they met with several men who had arrived in a Lincoln Continental with North Carolina license plates. The men in the Lincoln took several packages from the trunk and placed them in the trunk of the car in which Darby arrived. Darby then handed over some money to one of the men in the Lincoln.

The following January, Group 12 agents followed John Darby and an associate from Philadelphia to a bar in Brooklyn. Just past midnight, Donald Conner left the bar and drove off. Shortly after, Darby and his associate left the bar. The agents tailed them to 1365 St. John's Place in Brooklyn where they entered the building. About a half hour later, Conner, Darby and two other men left the building. Darby handed a package to Conner in the street.

There were many more meetings and exchanges of packages like these, and the feds were there to document the transactions. Uncle Sam was patiently building a strong conspiracy case against the associates Black Caesar had left behind.

As the hunt for Matthews intensified, investigators continued to find success in putting together their conspiracy case. A big break came when Walter Rosenbaum, Pop Darby's cutting materials contact, agreed to help prosecutors. On February 27, 1974, Rosenbaum introduced Darby to Benjamin Swint, an undercover DEA agent who posed as a corrupt security guard from a New York pharmaceutical house. Rosenbaum told Darby that Swint could get all the quinine his organization needed. Swint gave Darby a pound of quinine as a sample and Darby tested it. The sample met Darby's standards, and he agreed to pay Swint $2,000 per barrel. Arrangements were made to send the shipment to a Darby associate in New Jersey. On March 1, 1974, Swint delivered the quinine for $3,900 in cash. Later, Rosenbaum told a jury about this deal and all he knew about the Matthews organization.

Matthews' associates had more to worry about than just the surveillance by federal authorities, possible informant infiltration of their organization and attacks by rival drug gangs. At approximately 4:30 a.m. on February 4, 1975, Charles Swayzy Cameron and four companions left the Midway Lounge on Amsterdam Avenue and 123rd Street in

Manhattan. Cameron, a close Matthews homeboy from Durham who worked for Black Caesar's organization, was out of prison on $100,000 bond while he appealed a New York state narcotics conviction. Suddenly, four men, with guns drawn, approached them. Words were exchanged and a scuffle ensued. Cameron's four friends fled, although one of them, Anthony Foster, was injured during the attack.

Cameron was blindfolded, shoved into a waiting car and driven to an apartment that Cameron believed was in the Bronx. Over the next three days, Cameron was held captive in the apartment while his abductors threatened death and physically abused him. They punched his head and rib cage, inserted a hot pipe in his rectum and burned him with lit cigarettes. The abductors phoned Cameron's wife, family and friends and demanded a ransom of $25,000 for his release.

Cameron later recalled for police many details about his capture. The building where he was held was recently renovated. The lobby had a black and white square tile floor. The apartment's intercom system to the outside hall did not work. The kidnappers made numerous references to Muslim dietary laws.

The NYPD got wind of the kidnapping and launched an investigation. The police traced the ransom demands to 400 Herkimer Street in Manhattan, and they put the apartment under round the clock surveillance while they monitored incoming and outgoing calls. Then Laurence Feitell, Cameron's lawyer, called police to inform them that his client's $25,000 ransom had been paid. At about 5 p.m. on February 7, 1975, Cameron's kidnappers released him in the vicinity of Yankee Stadium. Bruised and exhausted, Cameron managed to find the apartment of his friend Sidney Hall's fiancé and called his wife.

The police picked up Cameron's call to his wife and sent several police officers to pick him up for questioning. Not knowing what to expect, the cops had their guns drawn when they asked Cameron to come to the precinct to answer some questions. An angry Cameron refused and expressed bitterness that the police had not done more to free him. But Cameron's wife assured him that the police had tried to find him, so he relented.

Roger Gray, a Group 12 detective, attended Cameron's interrogation at the precinct. "Cameron had a case of diarrhea of the mouth, but he took his attorney's advice and clammed up," Garay recalled. "But before he did that, he dropped a bombshell. We were taping the session but we didn't tell him. Cameron said: 'Look, I'm tired, and you guys know I'm a dope dealer. So what I want to do is go home.'"

Cameron had admitted he was a drug dealer. The tape would later be introduced in court as evidence against him. He had no plans, though, to stick around. He did his own disappearing act and became a fugitive from the law.

According to Rick Talley, a former drug dealer from the Matthews era, Cameron's kidnapping was not unusual. In fact, several prominent criminals were kidnapped and held for ransom. Some of the victims were even murdered. Cisco, a big-time operator and friend of gangster legends Freddie Myers and Pee Wee Kirkland, was a kidnapping victim. "Cisco got kidnapped twice," Talley recalled. "The first time it was for $35,000. Cisco had power in the hood but he paid up." Sam Hawkins was another kidnapping victim. "His kidnappers wanted $1,000, but Sam escaped," Talley recalled.

According to Talley, the kidnappings began with one gang, but then several gangs got involved once they saw how lucrative kidnapping could be. Still, not all the kidnappings were successful. "A gangster named Ivan and his crew were getting ready to kidnap Nicky Barnes," Talley said. "The feds were tailing Nicky. They realized what was going on and broke up the kidnapping."`

In 1972, a NYPD Intelligence Division report revealed how the kidnapping trend was playing out at both the street and kingpin levels. According to the report, "Law enforcement officers learned about more prominent street-level pushers. Because of the necessary exposure after these pushers began using girlfriends, wives and trusted friends to hold contraband for them. Some of the bolder addicts found it quite profitable to rob the narcotic holder. Occasionally they found that the drugs had not been delivered or picked up. This necessitated holding a hostage until the delivery had been consummated. Underworld characters began perpetrating robberies against major violators; their mills and the gambling games frequented by them became fair game. As the major violators became more security conscious, the hoodlums returned to the methods of taking hostages and demanding a ransom for their safe return. Kidnapping has now become a more frequent occurrence, and it's reluctantly accepted as an occupational hazard among major violators."

The kidnappings went on for about two years and led to several murders before the police finally clamped down and busted several of the kidnappers. "A lot of them dudes got life without parole," Talley said. "Some are still in jail. They're never getting out."

On February 22, 1975, a little more than 14 months after Matthews was arrested in Las Vegas and 46 months after the investigation began, the U.S. government announced the indictment of Black Caesar and his associates for conspiracy to violate federal laws. The feds charged that, in a conspiracy covering the period from September 1968 to January 1978, large quantities of heroin and cocaine were smuggled. Although the press had earlier identified John "Pop" Darby as a minor member in the Matthews organization, the indictment identified him as the man who oversaw the day to day operations after Matthews jumped bail. The feds made it clear, though, both at the press conference and in court, that Frank Matthews was the kingpin of the crime ring.

In announcing the indictment, David G. Trager, U.S. Attorney, said that federal officials were aided in the investigation by the police in New York City, Atlanta, Philadelphia, Newark, New Haven, Baltimore, Washington, D.C. and Durham North Carolina. He noted that in addition to Matthews, five other associates were being sought by the law: Gattis Hinton, Charles Cameron, Robert Currington, Scarvey McCargo and Fred Brown. Cameron and Walter Rosenbaum were charged in the indictment, but they pled guilty prior to the trial. Cameron was sentenced to 10 years imprisonment, given a special parole term of five years and fined $10,000. Rosenbaum, who testified as a special government witness, received three years' probation. By trial time, Frank Matthews and Gattis Hinton were still fugitives.

After a ten-week jury trial, five of the defendants were acquitted: Marzella Steele Webb, Robert Currington, Ernest Robinson, James E Martinez and Lucy Matthews. The eight convicted at trial (Barbara Hinton, William Beckwith, James W. Carter, Scarvey McCargo, Charles Swazzy Cameron, Thelma Darby and David Bates) were each sentenced to at least two years imprisonment, but they immediately appealed their sentences.

Barbara Hinton's legal counsel argued in court that her conviction should be thrown out because she was indicted by the same grand jury that heard her testimony under a grant of immunity. At the trial, Hinton took the stand on her own behalf, claiming she had nothing to do with the narcotics business and did not know that her common-law-husband, Frank Matthews, was a drug dealer. All she did, Hinton maintained, was stay at home and take care of the kids. On cross- examination, the prosecutor showed Hinton documents to refresh her memory and confronted her with wiretap evidence. She was evasive, claiming she couldn't recall a specific conversation from the wiretaps.

In one exchange, Hinton was questioned about a conversation she had on September 11, 1972. Hinton had called the Nostrand Lounge, a Brooklyn bar, and tried to reach someone named "Robert." The wiretapped conversation indicated that she knew Robert and had seen him earlier at the Nostrand Lounge. Hinton asked Robert if his guy would be ready. Hinton and Robert then discussed the fact that they were being watched by the police both from the front and the back of the bar at an earlier rendezvous. Hinton ended the conversation, warning Robert that he would have to be careful when they met that evening.

When questioned about the conversation, Hinton said she did not recall it. The recording was re-played to refresh her memory, but Hinton insisted she had never been to the Nostrand Bar, nor did she know a person named "Robert" with whom she was supposedly talking. Finally, she stated she had no idea to what the conversation referred or to what purpose the proposed meeting was set. Given the prosecutor's razor sharp questioning, Hinton gave a virtuoso performance. Still, the jury did not believe her testimony, and she was found guilty.

In the appeal proceedings before Judge Mishler, the prosecution argued that testimony of informant Donald Keno James and the wiretap evidence provided more than enough probable cause to indict. In explaining his decision, Judge Mishler noted, "Once a defendant has demonstrated that he has testified under immunity to matters relating to the federal prosecution, the prosecution has the affirmative duty to prove that the evidence it proposes to use is derived from a legitimate source wholly independent of Hinton's testimony." The judge affirmed all of the convictions save one. Nearly eighteen months after her conviction, Barbara Hinton walked out of court a free woman.

Today, former Federal Prosecutor William Callahan, who worked on the Matthews investigation, downplays the reversal of Hinton's conviction. "We lawyers are accustomed to reversals," Callahan said. "Hinton was never high on our agenda."

The trial was finally over. The Frank Matthews organization was now history, but its kingpin was nowhere to be found. The DEA continued to search the globe for the fugitive and had no doubt it would get its man.

# NINE

# THE DEA MANHUNT

*"We heard a lot of war stories about Matthews. It was good information, but a lot of what they talked about wasn't in the reports. How can you share information if it's not written down? While we stumbled along, the Matthews trail got colder."*
**Al Parrish, DEA agent**

SOON AFTER ITS creation in 1968, the Bureau of Narcotics and Dangerous Drugs (BNDD) came under heavy criticism for the corruption within its ranks. The corruption got so bad, in fact, that BNDD head Robert Ingersoll felt compelled to ask the CIA for help in ridding the Bureau of dirty agents whom he believed had ties to drug traffickers. To do that, Ingersoll wanted the CIA to help him recruit some thoroughly reliable people who could be used, not only as special agents in his various office around the country, but also as informants who would spy on the other BNDD employees, especially its top managers. Known as Operation Two Fold, the initiative is still a mystery because, as the Rockefeller Commission explained, "It violated the 1947 act, which prohibits the CIA's participation in law enforcement activities."

This move did not save the BNDD. On July 1, 1973, the day before Frank Matthews failed to appear in court in the Eastern District of New York and subsequently became a fugitive, Uncle Sam merged the BNDD and other federal drug fighting agencies into a new agency: the Drug Enforcement Administration (DEA). The DEA began with 1,470 agents and a budget of $75 million, but by 1975, those numbers had almost doubled. According to Douglas Valentine, author of *Strength of the*

*Pack*, "by 1977, at least 125 former CIA officers had infiltrated the DEA at every level of the organization, including its intelligence units." Some in Group 12 suspected that at least one in their ranks might be one of those infiltrators.

On November 5, 1973, about four months after Frank Matthews jumped bail, the DEA established the Central Tactical Unit 2 (Centac 2). Its purpose was to find Frank Matthews and capture as many members of his drug-trafficking organization as possible. Located in New York City on 57th Street, Centac 2 operated on the assumption that Matthews was alive, still in charge of his narcotics organization and still in contact with certain members of his organization, principally John "Pop" Darby. According to a Centac 2 directive, "around the clock efforts will be carried out to apprehend him (Matthews)."

Soon after its creation, Centac 2 contacted and briefed Interpol, Europe's leading law enforcement agency, thus making the Matthews investigation a worldwide manhunt. Interpol began reporting to Centac 2 that Matthews had been spotted in Rome, Amsterdam and some other European cities. The CIA was also contacted, and the agency assured Centac 2 that they would use their contacts in Venezuela and Latin America to find out all they could about Frank Matthews.

At this point domestically, the DEA was not getting much help from other law enforcement agencies. The U.S. Marshals had not yet joined the case. The IRS had stored in a warehouse potential evidence taken from Matthews' Todt Hill home, but Centac 2 could not get access to it. Having Matthews' photo and name added to the FBI's famous 10 Most Wanted List might have helped the manhunt, but in the mid-1970s, the bureau did not get involved in drug cases. "At that time, drug cases were the sole province of the DEA," Callahan explained. "Having the FBI involved with the case might have helped capture Matthews, but in those days, the FBI would have dragged its feet going after a drug pusher."

In addition to the manhunt for Matthews, Centac 2 was also responsible for building a strong legal case that could lead to conspiracy and perjury indictments in the Eastern District of New York and in Miami against key members of Matthews' organization. Their work on the legal case eventually led in 1975 to the indictments in the Eastern District Court in Brooklyn, New York of Barbara Hinton and the other members of Matthews' crime syndicate.

Approximately 15 DEA agents were assigned to the Centac 2 investigation, including some old hands from the Group 12 Matthews investigation: Gerry Miller from Group 12 of the New York Joint Task Force; Benny Smint, the undercover agent whom Walter Rosenbaum had introduced to Pop Darby as the man who could help the Matthews organization find cutting materials for its heroin smuggling operation; and Roger Garay, the NYPD detective assigned to Group 12.

Six of the 15 agents formed Centac 2's Fugitive Response/Apprehension Team that went out into the field and aggressively searched for Matthews. The two main members of that group were Al Parrish, who was reassigned to the team from his position as the DEA's Staff Coordinator of Enforcement in the Washington, D.C. office, and Glenn Chism, who was re-assigned from the DEA's Dallas, Texas division where he had worked on a fugitive task force. During the next year, Parrish and Chism would literally live and breathe the Matthews investigation. "I wore out two sets of luggage looking for Matthews," Chism revealed. " It was the biggest manhunt in DEA history, so it was exciting to be part of the team. But it was frustrating as well. It looked as if we had mountains of evidence, but as we moved forward, the leads seemed to vanish into thin air."

Parrish's and Chism's first task was to get up to speed with the investigation. So they spent countless hours reading reports, reviewing the background file on Matthews' friends and family members, checking out the phone tolls and identifying sources that might be willing to talk. The two agents were disappointed at what they found in the files: next to no useful intelligence and no real leads to Matthews' whereabouts. If the reports were to be believed, he could be in Africa, Philadelphia, Venezuela, Chicago, rural North Carolina, maybe Europe, or even Hong Kong. The Bahamas would have to be checked out because Matthews owned some property there, while Paraguay was of interest as research revealed that more felons where hiding out there than in any other country.

Strong rumors placed Matthews in Algeria, which would have been a good place for him to hide. Algeria and Uncle Sam were enemies, and the two countries had no extradition treaty. Tim Leary, Eldridge Cleaver, Stokely Carmichael and other noted 1960s radicals, as well as some Black Muslims, had gotten into trouble with the law in the U.S. and fled to Algeria. Black Caesar certainly had the money to buy protection, and he could have gotten along with the Black Muslims. After all, Matthews was a professed admirer of Malcolm X. A flaky radical like Tim Leary, however, might have been too much to take for a guy like Matthews. Algeria, moreover, had a rigidly socialist government, and an authoritarian political system that would not have appealed to the free-living drug lord. Centac 2 hoped Matthews would not be in Algeria because it would be next to possible to catch him.

As hundreds of leads poured into Centac 2 from all over the world, Parrish and Chism drew a sober conclusion. Matthews could be anywhere and nowhere. "During the entire time I was involved with the investigation, I never interviewed anybody who actually knew anything about Frank's whereabouts," Chism revealed. "They would say invariably that, if they knew where Frank was, they would not tell us because Frank was generous with his money."

And that was the big problem with the investigation— nobody was willing to give up information about Matthews. Parrish realized that people needed an incentive to stick out their necks. It was DEA policy not to give rewards, but Parrish had done research and discovered that a federal reward of $20,000 had been helpful in the apprehension of John Dillinger, the famous Midwest bank robber of the 1930s Depression. So why not a reward for Frank Matthews? Was not he supposed to be the biggest fugitive in DEA history? "I presented the idea to some of my colleagues," Parrish recalled. "They laughed and said the Justice Department would never approve it. Parrish sent a proposal to his supervisor anyway. To everybody's surprise, the $20,000 reward was approved, the first time the DEA had offered a reward."

It was not too long after they joined Centac 2 that Parrish and Chism were on the road to interview sources. "Barbara Hinton was one of the first people Parrish and Chism visited. By that time, Hinton had moved to 95th Street in Brooklyn. "We interviewed Barbara at her liquor store," Chism said. "The store was sparsely stocked, and it didn't look to be a money maker. Barbara struck me as being bitter. I don't know if she was that way personally or if she was upset that Frank had left her. In any case, we believed she didn't know anything."

After interviewing Hinton, Parrish left, thinking Matthews could be dead. "It did not seem that Hinton had any recent contact with Matthews," Parrish recalled. "What kind of man leaves his kids and doesn't show up again? Surely, if he was alive, he'd have stayed in contact with Barbara for the sake of the kids. I just didn't get it."

If Hinton appeared bitter, Matthews' Aunt Marzella was downright hostile and uncooperative when Parrish and Chism showed up at her Durham, North Carolina home. She complained to the two agents that they were picking on her nephew, and she refused to answer any questions. The agents were literally chased away. "Marzella doesn't really talk much today about Frank," one source who knows Marzella well revealed. "She never got over the fact that she was hauled into court as part of that (1975 conspiracy) trial."

Parrish and Chism went to Queens, New York, to interview Cheryl Denise Brown's parents, Gordon and Lorna Brown, but it turned out to be another fruitless visit. "The parents were distraught," Parrish recalled. "Cheryl's mother told us that, if she knew where her daughter was, she wouldn't tell us. That was the end of that. Then the father said that if we didn't leave them alone, he was going to get a lawyer and lodge a complaint." The agents tried to make the Browns understand that they were trying to find their daughter, but to no avail.

Even Cheryl's cousin in Queens got hostile with the agents when they showed up to talk to her. She could not understand why the authorities wanted to talk to her again since some people from the investigation had already come by the day before, and she had told him all she knew. Parrish and Chism were pissed off. Nobody had told them that an investigator would be coming to see the cousin before they did. It would not be the last time wires got crossed.

The agents were shocked at the nature and progress of the conspiracy part of the investigation. Enacted in 1970, RICO (the Racketeer Influenced Corrupt Organizations Act) was the statue that now made conspiracy investigations possible. But it was a new investigative tool, and Uncle Sam did not yet have the experience in how to use it effectively.

"The first successful drug conspiracy prosecution occurred in 1970 in a Texas federal courtroom before Judge Sara T. Hughes," Chism recalled. "I participated in the investigation. We were all new to the application of the RICO conspiracy law. We got a conviction, but the prosecutors confused the hell out of the jurors with their talk of conspiracy."

Parrish and Chism found themselves wasting time and having to help out with the conspiracy investigation rather than looking for Matthews. Moreover, agents working on the case did not like to write things down, and this frustrated Parrish and Chism to no end. "We heard a lot of war stories about Matthews," Parrish explained. "It was good information, but a lot of what they talked about wasn't in the reports. How can you share information if it's not written down? While we stumbled along, the Matthews trail got colder."

The agents were especially critical of Gerry Miller who headed Group 12's investigation of Matthews. According to Parrish, Miller thought he knew everything about Matthews, but the reports revealed exactly the opposite. For the most part, the reports contained information of little importance about the fugitive. The agents learned that Matthews may have been willing to cooperate with authorities and perhaps had even given up some important people with whom he had worked, but he had no intention of giving up his homeboys or the people in his organization. "Miller refused Matthews' offer," according to Parrish. "Miller wanted to get the brothers in Matthews' organization," Parrish said. "That was stupid. We already had them on the wiretaps. On top of that, somebody spooked Matthews by telling him he was going to get life. You never say that. Matthews must have felt as if he had no choice but to run."

Parrish and Chism never thought that the fugitive apprehension team was in control of their part of the investigation. "There was really a lack of coordination between its members, especially in handling leads about Matthews' whereabouts," Chism revealed. "We were always a day late and a dollar short in following up on leads."

The agents spent an enormous amount of time listening to the wiretaps, trying to get a picture of Matthews' personality and character. "He seemed like a nice guy, very smooth, well organized," Parrish explained. "I never heard anything on the tapes that suggested he was a violent person."

There were hundreds of hours of tape-recorded conversations between Matthews and key associates, such as Pop Darby and Mickey Beckwith, much of it, as Chism described it, "jive talk among friends." Matthews spent a lot of time rapping about women and bragging about his sexual prowess. "He rarely talked about his drug business," Chism recalled. "I can remember only one such conversation where Frank complained about his workforce and thought the girls he recently hired were too lazy."

Frank used code in his conversations. For instance, he referred to workers as "tomato pickers." Both John Darby and Nathaniel Elder had trouble remembering the code words to use when discussing business. "Darby was real funny," Chism revealed. "You could tell from listening to the conversations that he had been coached about the slang code to use on the phone to confuse the wiretappers. But he had a hard time remembering what words he was supposed to use. Right in the middle of a conversation Darby, would blurt out, 'Oh, I didn't mean to say that.'"

Chism did not get the impression that Matthews was an "ironfisted hardcore drug kingpin" in charge of a sophisticated drug-trafficking organization. "Everybody keeps saying how smart Frank was," Chism explained. "As far as I could tell, he was just another drug dealer hustling to make a buck from narcotics."

Since most of the talk was not relevant to the investigation, the agents had to listen carefully to the wiretaps. That was often a futile exercise. Centac 2 had spent nearly $15,000 to have the tapes transcribed, but they were poorly done. The transcriber simply did not understand what he heard on the tapes. "What we read in the transcript was not what was being said on the tapes," Parrish explained. "The transcripts were just terrible. They were speaking urban Black English on the tapes, and the transcriber missed a lot. Glenn and I could understand the conversations because we are African American, but the truth is—Centac 2 wasted its money; we wasted our time."

Trying to understand the tapes and getting their colleagues in the Matthews investigation to write down what they knew was a pain in the ass, but Parrish and Chism loved the traveling they did in pursuit of Black Caesar. A seemingly bottomless budget allowed them to travel both domestically and internationally to anywhere a lead pointed them. Venezuela, the Bahamas, Atlanta, Las Vegas, Miami, Barbados, Puerto Rico were some of their ports of call. "I had a lot of fun going all over the place," Chism said. "It was just like being in a James Bond movie. "

Many of their field trips were based on faulty intelligence, vague leads, miscommunication and sometimes just plain incompetence. Following up on one tip, Parrish and Chism rushed down to Miami where Matthews owned a house in a middle-class neighborhood. The agents could see the lawn had not been cut for many weeks. Newspapers were piled up in the yard, and the air conditioning in the house was running full blast. "It was obvious nobody had lived there for a long time," Chism said. The agents also visited Jekyll Island in Georgia, where Matthews had property. When they got there, the residence appeared to have long been abandoned.

Another tip took the agents to, of all places, Donalsonville, Georgia, a whistle stop with a population of about 2,800. Interestingly, the town is the site of the second largest mass murder in Georgia history. Three months after Matthews jumped bond, seven members of the Alday family were murdered by three escaped convicts and a 15-year old kid. The crimes were portrayed in the movie *Murder One*.

Why would a drug kingpin with Frank Matthews' tastes and lifestyle be hiding out in the rural South? In examining the telephone tolls from

Matthews' phones, Centac 2 had discovered the phone number of the local sheriff's office. Parrish and Chism contacted the Georgia Bureau of Investigation (GBI) to find out what was going on in Donalsonville. They learned that anytime someone committed a crime in Georgia, they would almost invariably flee to Donalsonville and find sanctuary at the mission of a charismatic local religious leader. The local sheriff, the minister and the head of the FBI in Georgia all grew up together and protected each other like good old boys.

"Actually we thought Donalsonville was a pretty good lead," Chism recalled. "Matthews had a lot of money and could easily have greased some palms in the town. So we were jacked up, ready to put the cuffs on Frank when we arrived in Donalsonville. We converged on the sanctuary with state law enforcement backup. A real bummer! It turned out that Frank was not there. It ended up with me getting into it with the local redneck sheriff. We didn't get along. I didn't like the way he talked to me. Besides, he was corrupt."

Another trip on Christmas Day, 1974, took the two agents to Matthews' hometown of Durham, North Carolina. Centac 2 had received information that the fugitive would be visiting two of his kids who were staying with Aunt Marzella. "'There must have been two feet of snow on the Durham streets that day," Chism recalled. "We almost froze our asses off. Al and I huddled up in one vehicle, and we had to run the engine periodically to keep warm. Then we ran out of gas. We sat there all day wishing we were home. No visitors showed up. Come to think of it, Frank would have been stupid to come back to Durham. We did a lot of things like that."

It was not the last time Parrish and Chism went to North Carolina. "I talked to one guy who grew up with Matthews," Chism said. "The man got a call from Frank after Frank had been in New York City for about a year. Frank told this guy he was getting rich. The guy told us he thought Frank was just bullshitting him to impress an old homeboy." The agents found information like this interesting, but it did little to move the investigation forward.

And then there were some leads that seemed too good to be true. The investigators got excited when they received a tip that Cheryl Brown's parents were planning a cruise that would take them to a stop in Caracas, Venezuela. Agents thought it odd that the Browns would be taking a trip to one of Matthews' prime destinations so soon after their daughter had disappeared. "My supervisor told me that we had gotten intelligence that Matthews was hiding in Curacao where he had gotten close to members of the local police force and that, for whatever reason, he was planning to visit Caracas," Parrish explained. "We had no agents in Curacao, but I was planning a trip to Jamaica with my family, and my supervisor wanted me to go to Curacao and stay for a couple of weeks to check out the Matthews lead. He said I could take my family with me. It would be a good cover.

"I said to him, ' Yeah, my family would be good cover, but the minute I arrive in Caracao and start telling people about Matthews, my trip becomes official, and everybody there will know what I'm doing. I didn't like that happening while my family was there. So I went to Jamaica instead of Curacao. Soon after that, I completed my assignment with Centac 2. I don't really know if the DEA followed up and sent some agents to Caracao to look for Matthews."

Not all the leads were fruitless. One of the objectives of Centac 2 was to put Matthews' associates in jail. Since Black Caesar's flight, some of his associates had become fugitives from the law. Nate Elder was one of them. The Task Force learned that Elder was back in Atlanta hiding out at a friend's two-story townhouse. Parrish and Chism hopped a plane for Atlanta and put the townhouse under surveillance. It was not too long before Nate Elder arrived and entered the townhouse. The agents approached the townhouse and rang the doorbell. A black woman came to the door.

"We are special agents with the DEA," said Parrish, as he and Chism flashed their badges. "Tell Nate Elder to come to the door."

The woman tried to look surprised. "Nate who? I never heard of him."

"Come on, we saw him go in," Chism said.

The agents showed the woman the arrest warrant and marched in. They positioned themselves at the bottom of the stairs that lead to the second floor and drew their guns.

Al Parrish commanded, "Nate Elder, this is the DEA. We got a warrant for your arrest. Come down here now!"

Elder said, "Man, you say who?"

Chism bellowed, "The DEA!"

There was a pause, then Elder said, "Ok. Ok. Lemme get dressed."

"Come down here before you get your ass shot," Parrish said.

Elder appeared at the top of the stairs. He was in his underwear. The agents handcuffed him. When they went to the bedroom, the agents found a .45 caliber handgun on the nightstand.

"Elder had a reputation as a hard ass," Chism recalled. "Fortunately, we didn't have to shoot him. We interrogated him about Matthews' whereabouts, but he stonewalled us."

The most interesting experience that Parrish and Chism had with Centac 2 came on January 28, 1974, when they were both assigned as part of a team of agents to find Matthews at the Muhammad Ali-Joe Frazier fight at Madison Square Garden, New York City. It was the second of three fights between Ali and Frazier in what has been called the greatest rivalry in boxing history. Neither Ali nor Frazier were champs, but they were both hoping a victory would get them a fight with world champion George Foreman. Matthews was a huge boxing fan and Muhammad Ali was his idol. Centac 2 received a tip that Matthews had plastic surgery and would be attending the Ali-Frazier II in disguise. A crowd of more than 20,000 watched Ali win a hard fought decision.

"I was really excited," Chism revealed. "I was going to an Ali-Frazier fight and catch a big fugitive, too. The experience was really something for a young agent like me."

The agents arrived early so they could check out the crowd as it streamed in through the entrance gate. When they began taking photos, some NYPD detectives came over to Parrish and Chism and wanted to know what they were doing. Parrish did not like their attitude. He told the cops that he and his partner (Chism) were on assignment and to let them do their job. After the fight, a couple of the NYPD detectives came over to Parrish and Chism as they sat in their car watching the spectators leave the Garden. "One of the cops started to mouth off," Parrish recalled. "He reached into the car and I rolled up the window, catching his arm. He struggled to get free. I told him, 'Don't reach into my car again!' Then I opened the window to release his arm and drove off."

Parrish and Chism traveled to Las Vegas to interview a bellboy at the Sands Hotel. A tipster had told Centac 2 that Matthews was close to the bellboy and that he had received large tips from Matthews in return for arranging "dates" for him with prostitutes. He might know something about Black Caesar and what he was doing in Las Vegas. "The bellboy was cooperative until we asked him if he knew where Matthews was." Parrish recalled. "He snapped at us: 'Why should I cut off the hand that feeds me?' He never gave us anything."

While in Las Vegas, the agents also talked to the casino staff at the Sands about Matthews' gambling. "I got the impression from talking to them that Matthews had a gambling addiction and that is why he spent so much time in Vegas," Chism said.

The agents also suspected that Matthews may have been using his losses to launder money through the casinos, but Centac 2's job was to find Matthews, not to investigate the money trail. "Nobody in the government seemed interested in pursuing that money laundering angle," Chism recalled.

After a year, the DEA closed down Centac 2, and the U.S. Marshals assumed responsibility for the Matthews investigation. In reflecting upon their experience with Centac 2, Al Parrish and Glenn Chism both expressed strong feelings. They had spent enormous amounts of time doing research, examining evidence and traveling around the country and overseas, tracking down leads. Yet they had absolutely nothing to show for their hard work. At the end of the investigation, they knew as much about Matthews' disappearance as when they started.

"We felt we had wasted our time and had gotten nowhere," Chism concluded. "The DEA didn't have its act together." Parrish also expressed his frustrations. "The Marshals were trained to hunt fugitives. They are good at it. But when we left Centac 2, we really had nothing to give them. The Marshals were essentially starting over. "

Even though the Marshals took over the investigation, the DEA kept the Matthews case open, and the agency continued to look for any leads that might lead to his arrest and capture. With time, however, the leads grew increasingly fewer in number. By the 1990s, a new generation of DEA agents was on the job, and while they might have known of Matthews, they had little interest in his case. The DEA had other priorities.

Lew Rice joined the DEA in 1974 when the hunt for Matthews was in full swing, and he took a keen interest in the drug kingpin's story. "When I joined the force, there was a lot of talk about Matthews within the agency," Rice recalled. "I found it amazing that Matthews was just 29 years old when he jumped bail. Yet, he had dominated the heroin trade. In fact, he exhibited the leadership skills of a CEO. Still, he was a criminal and we have to keep his legacy in perspective. He sold heroin that destroyed thousands of lives."

The City of Brotherly Love had been one of Matthews' biggest markets, and until he jumped bail, his organization had a big presence there. Rice knew that, and he decided his office would keep an eye out for possible leads on Matthews. Every time the DEA's Philly office arrested a drug defendant, he would be asked a series of questions: Have you heard of Frank Matthews? If so, what have you heard? Is he alive? Have you seen him? "Our experience taught us that criminals usually are willing to cut a deal to reduce their jail time," Rice explained. "But you have to be extremely careful not to ask leading questions. You don't want to implicate and arrest the wrong person."

Most of the leads turned out to be dead ends, but on one occasion, the Philly office detained a suspect who appeared to resemble a 20-year year old photo of Black Caesar. It was difficult to be certain, though, because of strong rumors suggesting Matthews had extensive plastic surgery. The DEA had a tough time connecting the suspect to a fugitive who had been on the run for 20 years. Rice questioned the suspect about New York City and his time in Philly and how he lived and worked. "There were a few of the old time New York agents working in the office, and we had a spirited debate about whether or not we would detain this person overnight until a final determination was made," Rice recalled.

The office buzzed with the possibility of an arrest of a major drug fugitive. However, the excitement ended after the DEA had a FBI fingerprint examiner compare the suspect's fingerprints with those on file for Matthews. He was not the DEA's man.

In 1997, Lew Rice was transferred to the DEA's New York City office as a Special Agent in Charge. As the DEA's largest operational office, the New York posting is considered a flagship assignment within the DEA, and Rice was pleased to be given his new responsibility His career had come full circle. Rice had started in New York City, and he would end his career there.

Given the power of the New York media, Rice thought it would be a good time for the DEA to make another concerted effort to find Matthews. Rice engaged the services of noted forensic sculptor Frank Bender to make a bust of Frank Matthews. Bender had created a bust of Mob boss Alphonse Persico for the FBI and achieved national fame when his uncanny sculpture of New Jersey mass murderer John List resulted in his arrest in 1989 for the murder of his family. Using all the available information on Matthews' habits, background and family history and taking into consideration the stress he must have experienced from living a life on the run, Bender created a bust of the fugitive. The bust was put in the DEA Command Center so that agents could see it and be reminded of Matthews when they held meetings. Rice's DEA New York office also increased the reward for information leading to Matthews' capture to $50,000.

To spark interest in the story, Rice did several TV and newspaper interviews where the Mathews bust was on display as he recounted the Matthews story and investigation. The DEA task force group that Rice assembled to work the Matthews case made several trips to North Carolina and conducted surveillance debriefings. "The task force members included some of the more experienced narcotics agents who knew New York City," Rice recalled. "They didn't find Matthews, but if you spoke to those agents today, I think they would still say he was alive."

The DEA agents and police officers familiar with the Matthews story retired a long time ago. Rice, himself, retired in 2000. The DEA today is focused on the latest generation of drug traffickers. What does this mean for the investigation 40 years after Frank Matthews disappeared? According to Lew Rice, "The Frank Matthews investigation is still open and the DEA continues to look for him."

# TEN

# THE MARSHALS TAKE OVER

*"If Matthews had $20 million when he left and if he was still alive, what was his son doing stealing cars? I didn't feel that Frank had reached out to his family since he disappeared."*

**Mike Pizzi, U.S. Deputy Marshal**

THE U.S. MARSHALS Service (USMS) is the U.S.'s oldest federal law enforcement agency, tracing its beginning to September 24, 1789, when President George Washington appointed the first 13 U.S. Marshals following the passage of an act of Congress. The USMS was the principal federal enforcement agency of the 18th Amendment (ratified in 1919), which prohibited the manufacture, sale and transportation of intoxicating beverages. During the 1950s and 1960s, the USMS also provided security for the enforcement of federal laws and orders relating to civil rights. By the 1970s, the USMS had assumed responsibility for the apprehension of federal fugitives, which included Frank Matthews.

The USMS had always been the repository for all federal warrants. In fact, most warrants are first issued to the USMS and then the names of other appropriate agencies are added to the warrants as necessary. In the fall of 1974, the Frank Matthews fugitive case was just one of more than 1,000 such fugitive case files that the DEA transferred from its custody to the Marshals. "The USMS has always believed that a criminal who failed to appear in court is a priority, no matter who he or she is, and we are dedicated to pursuing them in support of the courts," explained Mike

Pizzi, a retired U.S. Deputy Marshal who oversaw the Matthews investigation from 1974 to 1989.

Pizzi had worked in trucking and construction before joining the U.S. Marshals in June 1965. He was first assigned to the Southern District of New York and then transferred in 1968 to the Brooklyn office of the Eastern District of New York. By 1974, Pizzi was the supervisor of the Fugitive Squad, with additional responsibility for the Federal Witness Protection Program and the Anti-Air Piracy Program.

Like many deputy marshals in the USMS, Pizzi wore more than one hat. The deputy marshals assigned to the Matthews case spent a great part of their day doing a variety of duties, such as court work, witness protection and prison transport and processing. The Marshals, in fact, worked the Matthews case in their spare time or tried to squeeze it in before or after their court work. Sixteen hour days were common for deputy marshals during the period the USMS began handling the fugitive cases transferred from the DEA. The truth was that the Marshals had little or no time or resources for the long term, expensive manpower-consuming investigative work that a case like the Frank Matthews investigation demanded. The sober reality—as the USMS plodded ahead, Matthews had plenty of time to make his trail even more difficult to follow.

The USMS knew that Frank Matthews was "The Man," the most prominent DEA fugitive, the biggest drug trafficker in the U.S., who had jumped bail in July 1973. The warrant for his arrest was finally issued on January 2, 1974. Black Caesar's capture after so many years on the run would be an important victory in the War on Drugs, as well as a feather in the cap of the USMS.

From the outset, the Matthews case was a tough challenge. The DEA is good at investigating drug trafficking, not finding fugitives. "The DEA wasn't trained to find fugitives," explained Dave O'Flaherty, who served as U.S. Deputy Marshal for the Eastern District of New York at the time the Matthews fugitive case was turned over to the USMS. "That's not their job. It had nothing to do with their professionalism."

O'Flaherty attended Albert Lea College in Albert Lee, Minnesota and the U.S. Army before joining the U.S. Marshals in 1971. During his 27-year USMS career, O'Flaherty received 20 U.S. Department of Justice special achievement awards and 200 commendations from federal, state, local and foreign law enforcement agencies. From the mid-1970s to the mid-1990s, O'Flaherty and Mike Pizzi, his supervisor, would be the two principal Deputy U.S. Marshals assigned to finding Frank Matthews.

The 1,000 fugitive case files the USMS received from the DEA were incomplete, sketchily documented and sometimes misleading. Pizzi would find himself looking for a fugitive who was simply named in the file, "One-eyed Louie." No first or last name was given. The file indicated One-eyed Louie was from Jackson Heights. He is 5'7" tall, 27 years old... a white male. No photo or ID available. The description could have fit a thousand white males in Jackson Heights.

The Frank Matthews case file was no exception. The DEA had done its best to find him, but the reports in his file contained little concrete information. Sources would not talk, despite a $20,000 reward, and virtually all leads turned out to be dead ends. Sightings of Matthews had been reported in at least 50 countries and several U.S. cities, but none of them checked out. Remarkably, as far as the DEA was able to ascertain, no one had seen Matthews since he jumped bail. The bottom line— it looked as if Matthews had disappeared without a trace.

The USMS began their search for Matthews with a sense of urgency and a 'in your face" strategy. They undertook surveillance of Barbara Hinton's house in Brooklyn but did not try to make their surveillance discreet. Every bar and nightclub Matthews frequented was put under pressure. It was not going to be business or life as usual for the Matthews family or Black Caesar's homeboys. "We spent countless hours pursuing and harassing everyone we thought knew Matthews or who had contact with him," Pizzi explained. "Some people were hassled to the point that they found it necessary to change their locations. Others got used to seeing us on a regular basis, and they didn't like it."

But the in-your-face strategy had its limits. Eventually, the USMS had to evaluate whether the strategy was working and whether the application of scarce resources allocated to it for the investigation was ever going to show results. "We never got anywhere with that strategy," O'Flaherty conceded. "We didn't shake up anything. We'd ask someone, 'Did see you see Frank?' They'd try to play us. They'd say, 'Got some money, brother? I'll tell ya.' We concluded that nobody we talked to knew anything and that Frank Matthews was no longer in New York City."

The USMS treated the Matthews case as high priority for about three years after it was transferred from the DEA. But in the late 1970s, the international drug trade exploded. Cocaine became a drug of choice for U.S. drug consumers, and the power of the drug trafficking organizations shifted from the U.S. to the international scene, particularly Colombia and Mexico. The USMS was now pursuing a new breed of fugitive, and the Matthews investigation was no longer a high priority.

By the late 1970s, the USMS may not have been as aggressive as in the early days when the DEA transferred the Matthews files, but they still diligently checked out every lead they received. In 1978, John Johnson, a well-known television personality in New York City, approached the NYPD with information about Matthews. Given Johnson's stature and credibility, it was a lead that the NYPD felt was worth pursuing. Born in 1938, Johnson was a respected ABC network correspondent, covering such important issues as the Attica Prison riot before joining New York television channel's WABC in 1972. The broadcast journalist became one of the first African-Americans to be inducted into the prestigious Director's Guild of America. By 1978, Johnson had been a well-known and visible fixture in New York City for many years.

Johnson told the NYPD that while vacationing in the Bahamas, he had been in a bar when a young well-dressed black man walked in with a woman on each arm. Johnson recognized the man as Frank Matthews, fugitive. According to the newsman, Matthews recognized him as well. After all, how many prominent black newsmen were there in New York City in the early 1970s?

The NYPD paid great credence to Johnson as a source since he was a professional journalist, and one would think, not prone to spinning tall tales. The NYPD alerted the USMS. Still, Pizzi was not so sure about Johnson's story. "I didn't think much of Johnson's reported sighting," Pizzi recalled. "Johnson was an experienced reporter who knew that he should contact the DEA or the USMS, not the NYPD. "

So why did Johnson contact the NYPD? According to Pizzi, "I think he needed something from the NYPD, and he used the story about Frank Matthews to gain favor with them." The USMS did check out the Johnson lead in the Barbados but found nothing.

In 1982, law enforcement sources in Houston, Texas, told the FBI that two fugitives, Frank Matthews and Cheryl Denise Brown, along with a man named John Darby, were in the city at the home of a Reverend Henderson. The USMS had already received a piece of mind- blowing information from a woman friend of Matthews. Black Caesar was in Houston, Texas, to have a heart transplant. The woman was convincing. The report seemed credible, the Marshals believed, because Matthews was said to have an irregular heartbeat, a condition that could be aggravated by heavy cocaine use, a habit of his prior to his jumping bond. Pizzi and O'Flaherty headed to Houston to investigate. They visited every hospital in the Houston area and reviewed hundreds of hospital patient records, attempting to find Matthews under an assumed name. But no luck. They never did discover anything that could verify if Matthews was or had been in Houston.

The investigation dragged on slowly though the 1980s as the leads dried up. The deputy marshals made the obligatory interview of the Browns, the parents of Cheryl Denise Brown who were now living in Florida. But the deputy marshals left the couple convinced that they knew nothing about their daughter's whereabouts or had been contacted by her. This assessment was reinforced by a wiretap that was put on the Browns' phone. Not once did the parents receive a call from their daughter or anyone else speaking on her behalf.

In the late 1980s, the USMS began paying more attention to the family Black Caesar had left behind. The three sons (Frank Jr., Shawn and Andre) had attended the prestigious Staten Island Academy when the family lived in Todt Hill. According to Keith Diamond, the family tutor, the children were well-behaved and doing well in school. Life held great promise for the boys.

When Pizzi and O'Flaherty interviewed Frank Matthews Jr. at Riker's Island in 1989, much had changed. Frank Jr. was in prison on a car theft charge. Surprisingly, he talked freely about his family. Brother Andre was living in Albany, New York, and having drug problems. Shawn was in Cincinnati with his mother, Barbara Hinton, who was living with her boyfriend Bud, who owned a bar. Junior talked nostalgically about how, when he was young, he would go with his family to Durham, North Carolina, to visit his father's Aunt Marzella.

He shared some family gossip. Marzella's daughter Peaches was driving around Durham in a new Mercedes Benz. To the deputy marshals, Frank Jr. appeared envious, but they let him talk on, hoping he would eventually spill a family secret or two. Junior told the deputies that the babysitter lived in Brooklyn, and that she may know where his father is. Junior did not explain why the babysitter would be privy to this information. The deputy marshals left the interview believing that Frank Jr. had not seen his father since he jumped bail.

Mike Pizzi also found the interview puzzling. He knew Mathews had been a good father when he was a kingpin, and his kids were taken care of. So why would Matthews just abandon his children and never see them again, not worrying about their welfare, even when their lives appeared to be unraveling? "If Matthews had $20 million when he left and if he was still alive, what was his son doing stealing cars?" Pizzi said. "I didn't feel that Frank had reached out to his family since he disappeared."

The USMS decided to focus on Cincinnati, Ohio, to see if Matthews was in touch with Barbara Hinton. The USMS alerted the Cincinnati police and began doing an investigation in Ohio and neighboring Kentucky. "What I knew about Kentucky told me that people jumped across state lines between Ohio and Kentucky if for no other reason than to avoid the harsh drinking laws of Kentucky," Pizzi explained. "So we thought it would be a smart move to search on both sides of the Ohio-Kentucky border."

The Cincinnati investigation did not turn up a family connection to Frank Matthews, but the Marshals did get some other leads. Sources claimed that Matthews was in France in 1976 and in Poughkeepsie, New York, in 1979 and that he had worked as a maintenance man at the Tree Pine Sanitarium in Vermont in 1985 and at a New York City nightclub two years later. These leads appeared to the Marshals as long shots, but they took the time to check them out. Still, none of them panned out.

In 1989, the USMS learned that Matthews associate Donald Conner was out of prison, and they decided to pay him a visit. Conner was cooperative and provided some interesting information, although a lot of it was not relevant to the Matthews investigation. Conner claimed that corrupt lawyer Gino Gallina, who was murdered in Greenwich Village in 1977, had swindled Barbara Hinton out of the money she had after Matthews jumped bond. Conner confirmed that he took Matthews to the airport the day he left town and claimed he gave Matthews what he told Groups 12 investigators more than 15 years before. He gave his draft card to Matthews to use as ID. The Marshals wondered: If Conner was speaking the truth, then how well planned was Matthews' escape? It seemed that the more they investigated the Matthews case, the less they knew about the fugitive. Then Conner dropped a bombshell. Conner told them that he had not seen him since his departure and he believes Matthews is dead. Conner did not give a reason why, but he did not appear to be lying.

If Black Caesar was still alive, with whom was he talking from his past life? Not one lead in the 15-year investigation had answered that question.

In 1989, the Marshals also interviewed Donald Conner's ex-wife Lorraine Foxworth who was living in Los Angeles. Foxworthy claims that she had not seen Matthews in 20 years, but she heard rumors that he was dead. Sources kept saying Matthews is dead and they did not appear to be spinning an agenda. At this point, it would have been easy for the USMS to conclude that the reason why it did not have any credible leads or sightings of Matthews was because he was dead. But at no time during their investigation did the USMS consider closing the Matthews case.

Black Cesar was a fugitive with an outstanding warrant for his arrest, and he needed to be caught and put behind bars.

The USMS continued to receive leads, especially from sources in the Cincinnati area. In 1990 Cincinnati police arrested an informant who had provided them with reliable information in the past and had even helped them solve a cop killing. The informant claimed that Matthews had been in Cincinnati with a man named James Perry, but that Black Caesar was now married and had moved to Conyers, Georgia, where he liked to hang out in a nightclub in Marietta, Georgia, owned by a famous ex NBA basketball great. The Marshals were skeptical, but they had to check it out. After several days investigating in Georgia, the Marshals reached a familiar conclusion. The lead was a dead end. The Marshals received more tips with the same results. Matthews was in Paraguay, South America, claimed one source. He had a girlfriend named Mary Crenshaw and was with her in Highland Park, Michigan, claimed another. Who was Mary Crenshaw and why would Frank Matthews be living in the cold state of Michigan? The Marshals have never found the answers to those questions either.

In the late 1990s, an informant claimed that Black Caesar was in Bermuda and using a Muslim name and that his Aunt Marzella was helping him through a friend who made regular visits to Bermuda on her behalf. With the help of Bermuda authorities, the Marshals checked the telephone records to see if there had been any long distance calls between Bermuda and the U.S., particularly to North Carolina. They found that a phone call was made from the New Jersey phone of Marzella's daughter to a family friend in Pembroke, Bermuda. The Marshals also checked the flight records to see if Gordon and Lorna Brown, the parents of Cheryl, had flown or planned to fly to Bermuda. Then several weeks later, the Bermuda investigation reached a familiar conclusion. The Marshals found nothing.

That has been the story of the Marshals' investigation since Day One. After more than two decades of investigation, the Marshals' Matthews case was the case that had gone nowhere.

By the summer of 1996, Mike Pizzi had long since retired from the

USMS and Dave O'Flaherty was nearing retirement. Now the Chief Deputy United States Marshal for Eastern District of New York, O'Flaherty decided that the Marshals should make one more push to see if they could close the Matthews investigation. One afternoon, he showed up at the cubicle of one of the best young deputies under his supervision, Debra Nightwine, and put a box on her desk. O'Flaherty said, "This is the file for the Frank Matthews investigation, the biggest case I've worked. I'm taking you off all your other assignments, and I want you to close this case before I retire. This is the only case you will work on. Bring it up to speed."

O'Flaherty explained why he wanted Nightwine on the case. "She is a smart investigator who I knew would follow the leads wherever they went. I could have assigned the case to a more seasoned investigator, but I knew Debbie was hungry, dedicated and focused, and that's what caught my eye."

Nightwine had never heard of Frank Matthews, but she was excited to be assigned the case."Dave was my boss and mentor and I respected him a lot," Nightwine explained. "I could see how much the Matthews case meant to him. I really wanted to do a good job, so I dove right into it."

When Lew Rice, Special Agent in Charge of the New York City office, re-opened the Matthews investigation in New York City, Nightwine joined a special task force assembled for the Matthews case that included a DEA agent, a NYPD detective and a New York state trooper. Once again, at least for a while, the Matthews case became a multi-agency investigation.

O'Flaherty wanted Nightwine to investigate quietly and behind the scenes. He believed Matthews was alive and did not want the fugitive to find out what the USMS was doing. So instead of going out into the field and interviewing sources, O'Flaherty had Nightwine do background checks that involved examining bank records, credit card records, travel records and phone records. Were there any suspicious long-distance phone calls? Money transfers? Bank deposits? Travel by family or close Matthews associates to strange places? Nightwine investigated.

The Deputy Marshal also got a court order so she could examine the bank records of Aunt Marzella. She checked the financial records of Matthews' three children as well and was surprised to learn that none of them had any money and that some of them had been in trouble with the law. Barbara Hinton had remarried, but there was nothing out of ordinary with her finances. "None of the Matthews family or close friends had come into any money," Nightwine recalled. "Nobody seemed to be living a real comfortable lifestyle."

Then the USMS received a tip that Matthews would be in the Durham on Thanksgiving Day 1996 to see his Aunt Marzella. Nightwine and another agent spent three tiring days in Durham checking out the lead and conducting surveillance of Marzella's home. The Marshals had gone down this road before. Matthews never showed, and the Marshals found nothing out of the ordinary.

In 1997 the USMS began cultivating what it thought was a promising source. The source was in jail, but he had a female friend who was Marzella's good friend. He was willing to provide information about Marzella and her activities by snooping on his girlfriend. The source told the Marshals that he was sure Matthews was in Bermuda. He gave the Marshals the names of two individuals living in Bermuda who could be Matthews.

Nightwine spent a week in Bermuda looking into the informant's lead. She worked closely with local police and investigated the men whom the informant had identified as Frank Matthews. After a background check, neither of the individuals turned out to be Matthews. Still the informant had provided what Nightwine thought was a lot of useful information. She decided to continue working with him in the hope something would develop. Nothing ever did.

"The Matthews investigation was the most frustrating case I ever worked," Nightwine explained. "I literally worked the case 24-7. I followed through on every lead. By the end of the assignment, I began thinking that maybe the reason I didn't find anything solid was because Frank Matthews was dead."

After five years on the case, Nightwine left the USMS's Brooklyn office for a new assignment. The case was now under the supervision of Deputy Marshal Brian Taylor who had also worked in the USMS's Brooklyn office and had a lot of experience with fugitive cases. Taylor had even helped out Nightwine a little with the Matthews case when he could. Taylor took a good look at the Matthews case file and was stunned by how little useful information had been uncovered about Matthews after two decades of investigation.

He thought too much time had been spent investigating the Bermuda angle. "I would have been shocked if we found Matthews in Bermuda," Taylor said. "It was hard for me to believe that an African-American was hiding in a small ex-British colony, and he couldn't easily be found."

Taylor decided to take a fresh approach to the case. "I looked at the 1975 indictment and decided I was going to interview everybody who had been indicted in the case," Taylor said. "They all knew Matthews and had worked with him. Maybe after all these years somebody would be willing to talk."

People did not have to talk to Taylor if they did not want to do it. So Taylor decided that the best strategy to get them to talk would be to drop in on them at their homes or places of business unannounced. The element of surprise gave him a better chance that they would talk to him. Two of the associates he visited were close by and living in Brooklyn: Mickey Beckwith and Donald Conner. "Everybody I spoke to liked Matthews and every one of them said they did not know what happened to him," Taylor recalled. They were honest with us. They acknowledged that, even if they knew where he was, they wouldn't tell us."

Taylor went to Durham, North Carolina, to see Marzella Steele Webb and got the usual uncooperative response. But while in Durham, Taylor remembered that Gattis "Bud" Hinton, was a Durham native and had jumped bail around the same time Matthews had disappeared in 1973. Taylor decided to pay a visit to Hinton's mother to see if he could get her to talk about her son's whereabouts. While at the front door talking to Mrs. Hinton, Taylor noticed a man sitting on a couch, looking a lot like Gattis Hinton, or so Taylor thought. Taylor brought the man to local police station for finger printing. He turned out to be Gattis Hinton. The Marshals arrested him.

Taylor spent several hours interrogating Hinton. "It was the strangest interrogation," Taylor recalled. "Hinton denied everything. He denied knowing Matthews. He denied seeing him. He denied even hearing of Frank Matthews. We couldn't get him to tell us anything. We tried to reason with him and he stonewalled us. We got nowhere." Despite the lack of cooperation, the Marshals worked out a plea deal with Hinton, and he received a six-month suspended sentence.

Taylor worked the Frank Matthews fugitive case for two years. Like everybody else who worked it, DEA agents as well as colleagues, he had little to show for his hard work. "It was such an intriguing case," said Taylor, who is still with the USMS. "I wish I could be working on the case, even though I never did get any closer to finding out what happened to Matthews."

Today, the USMS's Matthews fugitive case remains open, but as time passes, the trail grows increasingly colder, making it questionable whether the USMS is still committed to finding Frank Matthews. A lack of attention would be understandable, given the USMS's workload. Each year the USMS must handle thousands of new fugitive cases, so why would a case 40 years old be special? In fiscal year 2011 alone, the USMS apprehended more than 36,000 federal fugitives and cleared approximately 39,400 felony warrants. This does not include the work the USMS does annually at the local and state level assisting law enforcement agencies.

My own experience on the investigation tells me that the USMS is not actively looking for Matthews. As a case in point, Barbara Hinton passed away in 2003, but nine years later, the USMS did not have this important piece of information when I came to the USMS's Brooklyn office for interviews. I got the information from the grandson of Frank Mathews Jr. and informed the Marshals of her death when Hinton's name was raised in a discussion.

I interviewed Charles Dunne, United States Marshal, Eastern District of New York, and he did not seem to know too much about the case, yet he claimed the USMS was still looking hard for Black Caesar. "Mathews may have fallen off the face of the earth, but if we get leads we will follow them," Dunne assured me. "We are still looking for the man from that famous prison break from Alcatraz."

Dunne was referring to Frank Lee Morris, an American criminal who escaped from Alcatraz Island Federal Penitentiary on June 11, 1962, and has been missing ever since. In the movie entitled *Escape from Alcatraz,* Morris is portrayed as a keen and brilliant mastermind of one of history's more daring prison escapes.

Dunne gave a couple of recent examples to make his point that the Matthews fugitive case was still active. Following up on one lead a couple of months before my interview with Dunne, the Marshals went to Durham, North Carolina, where they found a man who had the same height, age and facial features as Matthews, but who turned out not to be Black Caesar.

Dunne also talked about an investigation of a man from Bermuda who was the same age as Matthews and had done a lot of travel, especially from Bermuda to Charlotte, North Carolina, without having any visible means of support. The Bermuda authorities told the Marshals he was not their man, but the Marshals detained the suspect while he was in the U.S. and questioned him for hours. It turned out that the Marshals had interviewed him in the 1980s. No one had thought to take the suspect's fingerprints or listen to his voice. Remember that Black Caesar has a high- pitched voice, and that is a feature that cannot be changed by plastic surgery.

Dunne did not follow through. I left the Marshals' office wondering whether the Matthews fugitive case will remain an open investigation? Four decades after he jumped bail, there has not been a credible lead to prove Matthews is alive. No verified sightings. No snitches. No photos taken of him on the run. No fingerprints anywhere. Given the War on Terrorism and the era of tight government budgets, continuing to look for Matthews would seem like a waste of time and taxpayer's money.

The Marshals interviewed for this book said the USMS does not close cases when the subject is not found, even if the case may go on the back burner, as the U.S. Marshals admit this case has done. Retired deputy marshals who worked the Matthews case want to see the case given more intense attention.

"It should be presented to *America's Most Wanted* and other T.V. or radio shows, as well as billboards," O'Flaherty said, "Unless there is an all-out effort, we will never know what happened to Frank. I think an international effort needs to take place. Wanted posters can be sent to Interpol. They will then have a Red notice. A Red is an alert that law enforcement in foreign countries find useful. The USMS can also send Matthews' fingerprints to all foreign countries with which we have treaties, asking them to check their national fingerprint files against Matthews' prints."

According to O'Flaherty, these steps can easily be implemented. He explained, "If the USMS devotes the dollars, manpower and time, this would take about six months of organized work on the part of a team of about four deputy U.S. Marshals working full time on the case. As notorious as Matthews is, it's not asking for too much."

Yes, but is such a concerted effort still worth it? Even if Frank Matthews was captured or turned himself in, if he is still alive, that is, it is doubtful he would get any jail time. The records of the 1975 trial (the Unites States of America versus Barbara Hinton) are missing, and the National Archives has no clue where they are. Many of the witnesses who would normally testify against Matthews if he were brought to trial are dead or suffering from the ailments of old age, such as dementia or Alzheimer's. And as Marshal Brian Taylor put it, "What would be in it for the government to go to trial prosecuting a case more than 40 years old?" That's true especially if Uncle Sam and its CIA have something to hide in Venezuela about its relations with the Corsican Mafia and drug trafficking. Remember that nine of the people who were indicted in the fall of 1972 for supplying narcotics to Frank Matthews' criminal syndicate had the charges against them dropped because of their connection to the CIA.

If the law had the will and decided to try Black Caesar, legal experts say all that Matthews could get anyway is a couple of years maximum for jumping bail. They doubt that Matthews would be convicted on the conspiracy charge. But imagine the media circus if a legend like Frank Matthews gave himself up or was captured and brought to trial? Would the cost and attention be worth it for Uncle Sam?

Interestingly, the material arrest warrant issued for Cheryl Denise Brown at the time of Matthews' disappearance has elapsed. If she walked into a police station today, the authorities would send her home, not arrest her. One has to wonder, if Cheryl is alive, why hasn't she surfaced?

All of this theorizing, of course, is just idle speculation. Whether Frank Matthews is alive or dead is still an open question.

# DEAD OR ALIVE

*"Usually we had a piece of information or a lead that was solid, even in cases where the fugitive was now one month ahead of us or a state or country away from the last sighting or the last verifiable piece of information. But I don't recall a case from the past 40 or more years that involves a fugitive fleeing with a young girlfriend and both of them disappearing without a trace."*
**Mike Pizzi, U.S. Deputy Marshal**

**M**Y FIRST ENCOUNTER with the urban legend, Frank Matthews, came in 2006 while I was researching my book, *Gangsters of Harlem,* and looking for kingpins to profile. It did not take me long to decide to include a chapter about Frank Matthews.

Matthews had operated out of Brooklyn but spent much time in Harlem, and the narcotics he peddled had a devastating impact on the neighborhood. The more I researched the Matthews story, the more intrigued I became with him. He was certainly bigger than life—a country kid still in his teens who headed to the big city in search of fame and fortune and overcame many obstacles before becoming history's first African-American drug kingpin. Matthews dominated the New York drug scene long before Nicky Barnes and Frank Lucas made their impact. His reputation as a gangster soared to such a level that people called—or hailed— him "Black Caesar."

That would have been enough of a story to make for a great book about a notorious black gangster, even if it did have the usual ending for those types of books. In the typical pattern of the urban gangster story—those of the Nicky "Mr. Untouchable" Barnes, Frank "Superfly" Lucas and the Demetrius "Big Meech" Flenory—the kingpin would rise to the top of the underworld and spectacularly enjoy the fruits of their criminality, only to be invariably taken down by hubris, law enforcement and maybe drug use. Matthews' story, however, has a much different twist and another act that make it unique. Not only did Matthews become a drug kingpin, he also avoided long prison time by jumping bond and disappearing with millions of dollars and a beautiful companion.

I had read Donald Goddard's *Easy Money*, a good book that appears to be a biography of Matthews, but, upon closer reading, is more the story of Matthews' associate George Ramos. Most importantly, *Easy Money* provides virtually no information about Matthews' flight and disappearance. With that in mind I decided to update the Frank Matthews story.

Over the next six years, as I looked for leads, documents and photos that could help flesh out Matthews' remarkable story, I became, like everyone who delved into his life, obsessed. I thought surely there must be at least a few clues to tell us what happened to Black Caesar. Surely someone snitched for the reward and gave the authorities a credible lead on where he might be hiding. Surely, somebody must have bragged to authorities about having inside knowledge of Matthews' fate. Yes, it was difficult to follow the money trail in the 1970s, but surely the authorities must have a lead to some of the $15-20 million Black Caesar was believed to have stashed away before jumping bond. Surely a young woman like Cheryl Denise Brown must have gotten a little homesick and tried to reach out to her family and friends. Surely, at least one time. And surely Matthews' fingerprints, which are on file, must have shown up someplace, somewhere, sometime.

What happened to Matthews still remains a mystery four decades later; but disappearing in 1973, as Matthews did, was a lot easier than it is today. Computers had not yet become ubiquitous. The Internet was still the stuff of science fiction. Credit cards had just gone into wider general use. Airports did not have the screening that we see today. Just look at the way Matthews ostensibly fled. His associate Donald Conner claimed that after Matthews jumped bail, he gave him his own draft card to use as identification to board the plane. That Matthews could use that type of identification to get on a plane shows how shockingly lax airport security was at the time. Indeed, the U.S. Department of Transportation recorded 364 hijackings worldwide from 1968 to 1972, on average more than one hijacking per week.

George Wright was one of those hijackers who disappeared for nearly four decades until his arrest on September 26, 2011. Dressed as a priest and carrying a handgun in a hollowed out Bible, Wright was one of five Black Liberation Army members who went to the Detroit airport and boarded Delta Flight 841 for Miami. Wright "melted away" after being given safe haven in Algeria, which, interestingly, is the same country that some sources believe Matthews hid a few years later.

Wright and his fellow terrorists were able to board the plane easily because the screening systems in airports at the time did not require every passenger to be examined, only those who met a specific profile that the Federal Aviation Administration had in place. Obviously, George Wright did not fit the profile because he was able to get on the plane. So it is easy to see how a gangster like Frank Matthews would have been able to get on a plane with a draft card. It was not until 1973, the year Matthews jumped bond, that the FAA required U.S. airports to ensure that all passengers and their carry-on luggage be inspected before boarding.

How times have changed. Imagine Black Caesar jumping bond today and trying to stay on the run with a stash of $15-20 million (about $90 million in today's currency). We now have computer databases filled with all kinds of personal information and intrusive cameras, tracking our every move in the streets and on buses and subways.

A fugitive now has to be careful about trying to obtain and use a credit card. After all, Big Brother records and monitors virtually every detail of every transaction. Imagine trying to pay for a house or utility bill or trying to obtain a passport or use a cell phone. Good luck moving $15-20 million electronically without the authorities catching on. Of course, you can try to use false information –or even plant it to throw the authorities off your scent—but you had better know—or have somebody who knows—what you or they are doing.

Even though it was easier for a gangster to jump bond in 1973 than it is today, staying on the run, month after month, year after year was a remarkable achievement for the biggest American drug kingpin of the early 1970s. It was not because the authorities did not try to find him. As we have read, the DEA set up a special Centac Unit to hunt him down and then assigned six agents to accomplish the task. It was only the second Centac the DEA created. The first focused on taking down the five powerful families of La Cosa Nostra. The fact that the DEA was willing to offer a reward of $20,000, the biggest since the one offered for the head of Depression era bank robber and gangster John Dillinger, showed that the agency meant business.

The curious thing, though, is why the reward was never increased. An amount of $20,000 in 1974 was probably a significant amount of money at the time, but can the same be said for 1990, 2000 or 2012? Would a bigger reward help catch Black Caesar? It certainly would not have hurt.

Take the case of James Whitey Bulger, the leader of the Winter Hill Gang and FBI informant. He fled Boston in 1995 after being tipped off by John Connolly Jr., a Boston FBI agent who he was about to be indicted. During Bulger's ten years on the run, the FBI received numerous reported sightings of Bulger and his long time girl friend, Catherine Grieg, from all over the world, the U.S. and parts of Europe. In many of those sightings, the authorities could not confirm whether it had really been Bulger who was spotted or just a look-a-like. But unlike Matthews, they did have evidence that Bulger was alive. For instance, a video camera picked up Bulger at an ATM in Europe. Matthews, on the other hand, was spotted in more than 50 countries, but not one of those reports turned into a verifiable lead.

The FBI offered an attention grabbing $2 million reward for information leading to James Whitey Bulger's arrest and capture. The tip that led to Bulger's Santa Monica apartment and his arrest in June 2011 came from Anna Bjornsdottir, a former Miss Iceland. Bjornsdottir met Grieg one day when the two women took interest in a stray cat. Upon returning to Iceland from California, Bjornsdottir reportedly identified Bulger and his girlfriend to authorities after seeing television reports about Bulger and photos of Grieg. In this case, the reward was big enough to catch the Icelander's attention.

The authorities should offer a substantial reward for Frank Matthews if they are serious about apprehending him. A reward of a few hundred thousand dollars would certainly spark the public's interest in the case, but the authorities need to do more than that. As the Bulger case shows, they also have to bring attention to the case. That sizeable reward helped bring attention to the Bulger case. The DEA's New York office under Lew Rice's office increased the reward to $50,000 while re-invigorating the hunt for Matthews. But Lew Rice, the retired Special Agent in Charge of the DEA's New York office says today, "I don't know if the DEA would pay it (the reward)."

After Bulger had been on the run for 16 years, the FBI decided to launch a media blitz that alerted CNN and other major news organizations and media outlets about fugitive Whitey Bulger and his companion, Catherine Greig.

Unlike the Whitey Bulger investigation, the DEA or the Marshals have never brought the Frank Matthews case to the public's attention in a concerted manner. After Lew Rice had forensic sculptor Frank Bender do a bust of Frank Matthews in 1998, showing how the fugitive might have aged in 25 years, Rice then went to John Walsh's *America's Most Wanted* TV show to see if the producers would consider having a segment about fugitive Frank Matthews. Some fugitives have been caught just a few hours after their cases appeared on *America's Most Wanted*. The show, however, was not interested because Matthews apparently had not committed any murders for which he was charged. The case never aired on *America's Most Wanted*. Matthews has continued to stay below the public's radar.

Also, the Matthews case was never profiled as part of the U.S. Marshals less well-known but still effective 15 Most Wanted. The USMS established the program in 1983 to investigate and apprehend high profile offenders, including drug lords. Strangely, the program has an air of mystery. When I asked a deputy marshal what had to be done to get a fugitive on the Marshals Top 15, the response was, "You are welcome to use the FOIA (The Freedom of Information Act) and see if the Marshals will release the criteria. I just can't give it to you. Sorry."

According to reports, the list includes dangerous criminals, such as murderers and sex offenders who have a history of violence or who pose a significant threat to society. Current and past fugitives in the program have also included drug dealers and organized crime figures. For example, currently on the Marshal's Top 15 are Norberto Baron-Vargas, a native of Mexico charged with conspiring to manufacture methamphetamine, and Vicente Carrillo, a cocaine trafficker and money launderer.

The deputy marshals who worked the Matthews case said they discussed putting Black Caesar on the Top 15, but it never happened. Could it have made a difference in closing the Matthews case? Sources from the United States Marshals Service (USMS) are ambivalent. "Yes, possibly, it could make a difference because the Marshals would start a small task force (about four people) to work the case full time for a few months to see if they can develop any information," explained Dave O'Flaherty, a retired U.S. Deputy Marshal who worked the USMS' Matthews fugitive investigation.

Mike Pizzi, another retired U.S. Deputy Marshal who worked the case, was not so sure. He says Top 15 cases can be a real pain at times, given the steady stream of weekly and monthly reports deputy marshals have to produce and the bureaucracy they must maneuver through. Pizzi believes the task force would need to find some solid leads quickly or it would run out of steam. Pizzi added: "When we worked the Matthews case, we'd go to headquarters if we needed extra funds, and I don't recall that they ever turned us down. We got all the support we needed for the Matthews investigation without making it a Top 15 issue."

During my six years investigating the Matthews story, I got a good idea of the problems, frustrations and challenges that the DEA and USMS officials faced. Several sources I contacted thought, for whatever reason, that I was trying to find Matthews. I would explain I was merely documenting the Matthews story for the historical record while time allowed me to get access to the information, but many sources did not believe me. Some sources did have a good reason not talk to me. William Babe Cameron, for instance, had been a snitch and most likely wants to forget about the past. When I approached his house to talk to him, he was on a walker and did not look particularly healthy. As he left the house and leaned on his walker, he kept repeating the mantra, "Dead man walking, dead man walking." I don't know if he was referring to me, the author, or to himself, the snitch.

Another potential source whom I approached through an intermediary and who reportedly had close ties to Matthews, refused to talk to me at first. Then a couple of weeks later, the intermediary told me the man was willing to talk now. I asked the intermediary why he had changed his mind. He explained that the man had received a phone call from Frank Matthews, who was supposedly calling from Chicago. The man told Black Caesar that a reporter (me) was snooping around and wanting to ask questions about him, but that he had told the reporter through an intermediary he didn't want to talk to him. According to the intermediary, Mathews told the man, "You should talk to him. It's about time my story was told." Matthews must have changed his mind because the man who claimed to be in contact with Matthews never did talk to me.

During my research, I heard my share of strange tales about Matthews' appearances in Durham. One is the famous story about how, a few years ago, he appeared at a funeral dressed as a woman. Some local sources said that would be just like Pee Wee, the prankster, to dress like a woman and sneak into town. Other sources said, "Nah, Pee Wee was too macho to dress up as a woman, even for a joke." Two Durham sources even assured me that Matthews had had a sex change. A couple of homeboys claimed to have drunk booze and partied with Pee Wee at some of the liquor houses that still populate Durham, although how he could do something like that without it becoming common knowledge in a small town was never explained. And as one Durham source scoffed: "These dudes who claim to be with him weren't close to Pee Wee. You never hear his homeboys claiming to be in contact with him."

Some of the stories I heard reminded me of the Bermuda and Bahamas leads the U.S. Marshals pursued without success. One rumor had Matthews living in Bermuda and going down to Mississippi on occasion to meet his Aunt Marzella. Another rumor I chased claimed Matthews had a son while hiding in Bermuda and that the son was now attending North Carolina Central University in Durham. It was another lead that, once pursued, vanished into thin air.

It seemed everybody I interviewed has a good notion where Matthews is hiding. John Darby told Liddy Jones while they were incarcerated together that Frank was living comfortably in Africa. Deputy Marshal Brian Taylor said he had heard that Nigeria was the African country where Matthews was hiding. One DEA agent told me he heard that soon after Matthews fled, he had gone to Europe to have plastic surgery. A couple of sources in Durham told me that Matthews had a sex change. Former drug kingpin Big Head Brother Carter said he heard Frank had bought an island "somewhere." Group12 investigator Roger Garay believed that Matthews fled to Mexico for a while and then to South America, where he is today. "It is my firm belief that he is alive, although not necessarily with Cheryl," Garay said.

Gerard Miller, former retired DA agent, said the DEA had no verifiable information that Matthews actually fled the country. Retired DEA agent Lew Rice believes Matthews was too smart to leave the country and was actually living in the U.S. someplace where he could "blend" in, but many sources were sure Black Caesar was living quietly in the Caribbean.

Rumors abound about Cheryl Denise Brown, too. More than one source assured me that Pee Wee "had taken care of her" because a) she had become a liability or b) Pee Wee, the womanizer, had grown tired of her. Another rumor claims Cheryl is not dead but living quietly in California.

One of Matthews' homeboys even claimed that Matthews had told him how he had successfully managed to flee and disappear. Matthews had hooked up with another fugitive named Robert Vesco. *Forbes* magazine had ranked Vesco among the 400 richest Americans but listed his occupation as "thief." Vesco, who went on the run about the same time Matthews jumped bail, orchestrated one of history's biggest scams worth about $1 billion in today's money. In his ten years on the run, Vesco traveled from the Bahamas to Costa Rica to Antigua to Nicaragua and finally to Cuba in 1983. There he remained until his death in 2008. The homeboy assured me that Matthews had hooked up with Vesco to have the con man show him how to launder his money. DEA agents I interviewed are aware of the Vesco rumor, but they give it little credence. I agree.

I received several e-mails, mainly because of an article I had published about Matthews on the Crime Magazine web site. One of the e-mails came from a woman who claimed to be Matthews' illegitimate daughter. I had seen her name on some websites pertaining to Frank Matthews. Several of her relatives did not want her to talk to me, she wrote, but she was reaching out to me in the hope that I might have some new information about her father I would be willing to share. Deputy Marshal O'Flaherty confirmed her identity. I was hoping to interview her, but she must have taken her relatives' advice because she did not respond to my follow-up e-mail.

Another e-mail came from the son of George Ramos who explained his family situation, writing, "I had gone my entire life without knowing the facts about my biological father (George Ramos), whom I never met, or what kind of man he was. When I was 22, my mother finally decided to tell me that my father had been convicted of murder." Evidently, while in the Federal Witness Protection Program, Ramos murdered someone in Florida and had gone back to jail. The son had never met the father, but he kindly reached out to Ramos' relatives to see if they could contact Ramos to ask if I could interview him for my book. Ramos was not interested. Today, he is reported to be living in Louisiana.

After the appearance of "The Frank Matthews Story," a documentary I co-produced with Al "Profit" Bradley, one gentleman wrote me to inquire about getting a copy of the DVD. He explained that he was friends with the parents of Cheryl Denise Brown and wanted to see the documentary before the parents did, just in case there was something in the documentary that might upset them. I responded to the e-mail but heard nothing more.

I received several e-mails from people claiming to know Frank Matthews or from people, claiming to know people with first-hand knowledge of him. This one was typical, stating: "My stepfather was a close friend and partner of Frank Matthews. They were together in Las Vegas when he was arrested. He had wanted to talk to someone who can write the truth. He remembers dates, names and places. He went into the Federal Witness Protection Program many years ago. He is currently serving a couple of years at…"

One e-mail came from the grandson of Frank Matthews Jr. I responded, indicating to him that I had received e-mails before from people claiming to be related to Matthews, so how did I know he is who he says he is? He replied, "I am located in Cincinnati, Ohio, and so is my father, Frank Matthews Jr., the first-born of Frank Matthews Sr. I'm one of his (Frank Matthews Sr.) three grandchildren. My grandfather has another son, Shawn, but he is currently incarcerated. My Uncle Andre also lives in Cincinnati as well and whoever contacted you guys is not part of my family. No one really talks about my grandfather, but there is a lot of information that people do not know. If my grandfather is going to be out in public, I want to make sure he is presented correctly."

The phrase "no one really talks about him" caught my attention. Someone close to Aunt Marzella had also told me that she seldom mentions her nephew Frank. Some people might say, "Oh, they are not talking about Frank because they don't want to say anything that could get him arrested." I thought differently. If Frank Matthews was alive, would not family members be talking about him?

Maybe they don't talk about Black Caesar because he abandoned the family. Deputy Marshal Debbie Nightwine noted that her investigation into the finances of the people close to Matthews revealed that "nobody was living comfortably." The Matthews sons had begun life with great promise, the privileged sons of a multi-millionaire drug kingpin, but after the kingpin fled, their lives literally turned to shit, marked by drugs and criminal arrests. These developments would suggest that, if still alive, Black Caesar changed from a caring father to one heartless SOB. Would he make that transformation to stay free?

The more I researched the Black Caesar story, the more I began to debate in my mind whether Frank Matthews is alive or dead. At first, I assumed, like most people, that Matthews was alive and hiding out somewhere, keeping a low profile and enjoying his millions, with or without Cheryl Denise Brown.

One thing about Frank Matthews intrigued me as I investigated his story. He knew hordes of people and people, friend and foe, knew him and liked him, but I came to conclude nobody really got close to Matthews. Both Matthews' friend Joseph Sapia and homeboy Pete Thorp made the prescient observation that there was part of Matthews whom nobody knew and that he kept to himself. So maybe Frank could pull off a disappearing, not tell anybody and maybe never see anybody again, including his beloved aunt and three kids.

But the more I investigated, the more I began questioning that assumption. How could someone disappear off the face of the Earth without a trace? To say that had happened to Black Caesar is not hyperbole.

Not one of the hundreds of reports of his sighting has been verified. Matthews' fingerprints have never shown up anywhere. Not one snitch has stepped forward to provide verifiable information about Matthews' whereabouts. We really don't know what happened to him after he jumped bail. Did he hang around New York for a month, as detective Michael Bramble's report suggests? Did he go Durham and clean out a safe deposit box as IRS Agent Ron Taylor's report indicate? Did he hop a plane, as Donald Conner says? If so, where did he go? Did Cheryl Brown really leave with him? Moreover, how can two people leave together and both vanish without a trace unless foul play was involved?

Mike Pizzi believes that Matthews is dead because the USMS never did have a "substantiated" lead during its entire investigation. Pizzi elaborated, "Being the ultimate optimist, I originally believed we could find and arrest him. My deputies and I worked many cases where the investigation took us far and wide. Usually we had a piece of information or a lead that was solid, even in cases where the fugitive was now one month ahead of us or a state or country away from the last sighting or the last verifiable piece of information.

"But I don't recall a case from the past 40 or more years that involves a fugitive fleeing with a young girlfriend and both of them disappearing without a trace. Everyone makes a mistake, gets hurt, gets sick, misses home, misses funerals… but who can miss them all? Not Matthews. He was good but not perfect. No one is. Also, Matthews was flashy and loved to spend money. I know Matthews did not become a recluse, and Brown did not follow him into a monastery.

"Even if only out of curiosity, someone, somewhere had to be contacted. Sure, we heard rumors, but they never panned out. I believe that, if Matthews made contact, the word would have leaked out and eventually we would have heard about it."

Fugitives can get away with hiding for 40 years, but it's actually unusual for them to do that without leaving a trace if they are alive. The authorities normally have some kind of promising lead, no matter how slim. In the case of hijacker George Wright, for instance, a fugitive investigator with the New Jersey Department of Corrections working with the U.S. Marshals Service had a lead, but it took them nine years of hard work to develop it before they found him.

Interestingly, even if U.S. authorities find a fugitive abroad, there is no guarantee that the fugitive will be extradited to the U.S. Many countries do not have an extradition treaty with the U.S. In the case of George Wright, the Portuguese government has refused to extradite him to the U.S. because he is now a Portuguese citizen and has a family in Portugal. So suppose the U.S. authorities do find Matthews in a foreign country such as Venezuela. Well, that country does have an extradition treaty with the U.S. dating back to 1922. However it's riddled with ambiguities and contains an extremely limited list of extraditable offenses (e.g. bigamy). Moreover, even when the treaty does apply, Hugo Chavez (now dead) rarely cooperated. More than 70 other countries do not have an extradition treaty with Uncle Sam. Or suppose Matthews is a citizen of a country in which is hiding, Portugal, for example. Would that country extradite Black Caesar to the U.S.?

If Matthews is dead, what happened to him? That is as difficult a question to prove as is the corollary. If he is alive, where is he? Some people, like writer Seth Ferranti, believe that La Cosa Nostra killed Matthews. Ferranti explained, "I subscribe to the theory that the Mob had him whacked because he knew too much about their operation and also because, if he really had $20 million cash as the legend says, the Mob wanted that money for sure. Plus, Frank's organization was in shambles, and he was on the run from the feds. Whether arrested, indicted or in jail, Frank didn't have the juice he once had. So it was easier for the Mob to move on him. I believe that is what happened. Frank is swimming with the fishes somewhere."

But why would the Mob do it? Matthews had jumped bail, was gone and out of the Mob's hair. Besides, there are no rumors about the Mafia murdering Matthews, just speculation. As William Callahan, a former federal prosecutor who investigated Matthews explained, "No Mob informants have stepped forward to claim the Mob did it. That's unusual when the Mob is involved."

Indeed, the Mob has a tough time keeping secrets. Take the mystery of Jimmy Hoffa, the famous president of the Teamsters Union who served from 1957 until his imprisonment in 1967. On July 30, 1975, Hoffa went to the Red Fox Restaurant outside of Detroit to meet three men, two of whom were labor leaders and the other, a mobster. Hoffa arrived first, but none of the three other men showed up. Hoffa was last seen getting into a car in the Red Fox parking lot with several people. It is believed Hoffa never did get out of the car alive.

As one would expect, weird stories about James Hoffa's fate started to circulate soon after his disappearance, including one that had him skipping off to Brazil with a black go-go dancer. But all of the credible theories focused on the Mob, with mobster Anthony "Tony Pro" Provenzano fingered as the leading culprit. Tony Pro was the mobster who allegedly arranged the meeting with Hoffa at the Red Fox restaurant. As one union official said, 'We all know who did it. It was Tony and those guys of his from New Jersey. It's common knowledge, but the cops need a corroborating witness."

James Hoffa, by the way, is not the first mob-related disappearance. In fact there have been several. Canadian organized crime boss Rocco Perri became a big-time bootlegger after the Ontario Temperance Act of 1916 cut off the legal sale and distribution of alcohol. He eventually came to be known as "Canada's King of the Bootleggers." Perri disappeared in April 1944 in Hamilton, Ontario, and was never heard from again, and no body was ever found. It's commonly believed his body was deposited into the Hamilton Bay.

Louis Milito was a member of New York's Gambino crime family and a close friend of Sammy "The Bull" Gravano. On March 8th, 1988 Milito was called to a meeting at Louis Vallario's bar where it was reported he was shot in the head. Evidently, Molito had run afoul of Sammy The Bull. Milito's body was never found.

William Cutolo, who was also known as "Billy Fingers" and "Wild Bill", was a Brooklyn mobster in the Colombo crime family who played a key role in the 1991 to 1993 Colombo war. In May 1999 he disappeared after it is believed fellow mobster Alphonse Persico summoned him to a meeting. The Persico faction of the Colombo crime family feared that Wild Bill was going to make a power play for control of the family. Cutolo's body has never been found.

These three mobsters may have disappeared but unlike the mystery of Frank Matthews, it also widely accepted that they are swimming with the fishes or buried in concrete somewhere. Also, there are widely accepted explanations as to what happened to the three.

I believe it is possible Matthews is dead and could have been dead for some time. He did have an irregular heartbeat that could have affected his health as he aged and would have exacerbated by his cocaine use unless he got it under control while on the run. I was surprised to see the condition of the many Matthews homeboys who are still alive. Most are in poor health; some have to use walkers or respirators, with a variety of ailments, from diabetes to emphysema. It would not be surprising to learn that Matthews was in similar poor physical condition, if he is still alive. Remember, too, Barbara Hinton also died at a young age, in her mid to late 50's. Matthews was 68 years old as of December 2012, so it's not inconceivable that he could be dead of natural causes.

Some sources very familiar with the Matthews investigation believe that if Matthews was dead, his body would have shown up, or there would have been rumors of his demise. It is a lot easier to get rid of a body than one would think; for instance they have never found Jimmy Hoffa's body. Interestingly, some sources started to doubt whether Frank Matthews was still alive after viewing our documentary, *The Frank Matthews Story.* For the first time, our documentary revealed the Venezuelan part of the Matthews saga with its CIA—Corsican Mafia connection. Matthews' carelessness played a big role in the bust that broke up the Venezuelan connection and possibly jeopardized the CIA's interests in the region. A lot of powerful people in Venezuela, no doubt, were furious with Matthews and would have wanted him to pay for his screwup. Besides, he was a potential witness if he was recaptured.

If Matthews made it out of the country, he would have been far from his element and vulnerable, especially if he was traveling with a young woman. Rumors that Black Caesar had funneled $15-20 million out of country would have put his life more at risk. The CIA and/or the Corsican Mafia could have easily made him disappear without a trace. It has happened before and could have happened then."I began to change my opinion about Matthews after learning about his connections to the Corsicans and the CIA and to Rolando Gonzalez and Venezuela," Pizza explained. "Put all that together and put 10 or 20 million of dollars in cash in Matthews' hands, and I can see him headed for a hole in the ground without his money and with Brown right next to him. Matthews was no longer an asset, and as a fugitive, he was a liability. There was a big cash bonus that came along with his disposal. Why was Matthews valued in the first place? He knew how to deal drugs. But he could no longer put together any drug deals. If he lost or could not contact his former connections, what was his value? Zero. On the other hand, if he kept his contacts and continued to deal, someone would have heard about it in the last 40 years. And if they did, so would we."

Of course, the theory that Matthews was done in by the Venezuelan-Corsican connection is just that—a theory. As Ferranti said, "I could be wrong in believing that the Mafia killed Matthews. Who really knows? There is no solid evidence to support any theory, whatever way you look at it. It is all speculation at this point."

Many other people who were involved with the Matthews investigation believe—or want to believe—that Black Caesar is still alive, having pulled off the greatest disappearing act in crime history. Personally, I believe that Matthews is most likely dead. That is what I would bet on. But either way, dead or alive, no one really knows what has happened to Matthews. My guess is we will never know. With each passing year, it becomes less and less likely that any evidence will surface that tells for certain what happened to Frank Larry Matthews. The only sure thing we can count on is that the remarkable urban legend of Black Caesar will continue to grow and that we will not see a kingpin like him again.

Many individuals stepped forward and generously provided their time, resources and sage advice to make this book possible. First I look to thank those agreed to be interviewed for the record. They included James Aiken, Leslie Ike Atkinson, Al Bradley, Rich Broughton, Clarence "Shorty" Buse, Ron Caffery, William Callahan, Big Head Brother Carter, Glen Chisholm, Charles Clinton, Reggie Collins, Carter Cue, Ray Dearie, Joyce Diamond, Keith Diamond, Charles Dunne, Seth Ferranti, Carlos G., Roger Garay, Jimmy Harris, Pat Istorico, Ricky Johnson, Sterling Johnson, Liddy Jones, Joe Kowalski, Jack Lloyd, Norfleet Lucas, Gavin Matthews, Gerry Miller, Dave O'Flaherty, Gavin Matthews, Kenya Matthews, Debbie Nightwine, Al Parrish, Mike Pizzi, Bill Raewald, Lew Rice, Warren Robinson, James Olive Rowland, Joe Sapia, Skippy Scarborough, Rick Talley, Brian Taylor, Ron Taylor, Peter Thorpe, Andre Vann, Gaspar Vatrano, Bill Warner, Wayne Watson, Hank Wilson and Purcell Wylie

Several people provided photos and documents for *Black Caesar*. They include Al Bradley, Shorty Buse, William Callahan, Reggie Collins, Seth Ferranti, Dave O'Flaherty, Roger Garay, Pamela Harris, Liddy Jones, Debbie Nightwine, Dave O'Flaherty, Al Parrish, Mike Pizzi, Lew Rice and Warren Robinson.

Several people and institutions helped with research and arranging interviews, They include Bruce Bridges, Carter Cue, Pamela Harris, Carol Holder, Ricky Johnson , Amanda Mulvey at the DEA in New York City, Greg Plunges at National Archives in New York City, Lew Rice, Robert Ryals at the Dacus Library, Winthrop University, the Staff of the Durham Public Library and Jack Toal.

Thank you to Gina Dorman and Carol Herring for reviewing the manuscript and offering valuable suggestions and Seth Ferranti for writing the forward to this book.

Thank you to Dimas Harya and the staff at Strategic Media Books for putting the book together. I look forward to many future collaborations.

Finally, thank you to my wife, Magdalena, for her love, support and encouragement and helping to make my writing life possible.

## BOOKS

Botha, Ted, The Girl with the Crooked Nose," Random House, NY 2008

Cockburn, Alexander, and Jeffrey St. Clair, White Out, The CIA, Drugs and the Press

Ferranti, Seth, Street Legends, v. 2

Goddard, Donald, Easy Money, Farrar, Straus and Giroux, NY, 1978

## ARTICLES

DeMaria, Lawrence, "Drug king's effects sold for $5,085," *Staten Island Advance*, Jan. 12, 1974

Donsky, Martin, "Lawmen seek Durham man," Durham Morning Heraald, p. 1A plus, Nov. 10, 1974

"Eight convicted as members of drug ring for blacks" *The New York Times*, Oct. 9, 1975

"40 years later: Ali-Frazier an MSG classic," *CBS New York*, March 8, 2011

Harvey, Everett R., Matthews…quick connection put him in big time," *Staten Island Advance*, p. 1 plus

"Jimmy Hoffa, "Search: No sign of Teamster's boss remains in Michigan, *The Associated Press*, Sept. 29, 2012

Kramer, Marcia, and Arthur Mulligan, "18 indicted as members of giant dope ring," *New York Daily News*, Feb. 22, 1975

Kuiss, Peter, "Inquiry links a S.I. man held in Las Vegas to a cocaine ring," *The New York Times*, January 8, 1973

Perlmutter, Emanuel, "Moving of a drug suspect from Nevada sought," *The New York Times*, January 7, 1973

Recinto, Ron, "US deserter steps forward in Sweden explains 28 years AWOL "*The Lookout*, June 18, 2012

Seigel, Max, "Drug ring catering to blacks is termed broken in Brooklyn, "*The New York Times*, February 22, 1975

"$325,000 forfeit in drug case here," *The New York Times*, July 21, 1973, p. 28

Weiss, Murray, "Fugitive Kingpin Gets Special Kind of Bust," New York Daily News, August 14, 2000 p. 17

## GOVERNMENT DOCUMENTS

"Central Tactical Unit," Anthony S. Pohl to Daniel P. Casey, Memorandum, US Dept. of Justice, November 1, 1973

Commanding Officer, Liaison Section, Intelligence Division, to Executive Officer, Intelligence Division, Information Developed by Joseph A. Kowalski Resulting in the arrest of a major narcotics figure of federal authorities, Jan. 9 1973

"Frank Matthews: Summary of work session, DEA headquarters, Washington DC, Oct. 4 and 5, 1973

"Intelligence report," Coordinator, 13th Homicide Zone, to Commanding Officer, Brooklyn Detective area, Memorandum, February 12, 1975

Major interregional-international narcosis conspiracy case re: Frank Larry Matthews, 29 years of age," William P. Callahan to Andrew J. Maloney, Memorandum, January 31, 1974

Trager, David G, United States Attorney, to Honorable Thomas K. Meskill and al, Memorandum, Re: United States v. Barbara Hinton, docket No, 75-1402

United State of America v. Barbara Hinton et al., United States Court of Appeals, Nos. 1018,1019, 1023, 1062=1065, 1390, Dockets 75-1402, 75-1418, 75-1441-75-1445, 76-1024, Certiori Denied, Jan. 17, 1977.

## DVDS

"The Frank Matthews Story: The Rise and Disappearance of America's Biggest Kingpin," Strategic Media Books and August Media, 2012

"Ike Atkinson, Kingpin," Strategic Media Books, 2010

"Kingpins: The Freddie Myers Story," Pipeline Films, 2007

Ron Chepesiuk is an award-winning author, publisher, screenwriter and documentary producer, and director. He's a two-time Fulbright Scholar to Bangladesh and Indonesia and a consultant to the History Channel's Gangland TV series. His books include Sergeant Smack, Gangsters of Harlem, Gangsters of Miami, among others. He is also Executive Producer and co-host of the popular radio show Crime Beat (www.artistfirst.com/crimebeat.htm). For other books by Ron Chepesiuk go to www.strategicmediabooks.com.

# CURRENT AND FORTHCOMING TITLES FROM
## STRATEGIC MEDIA BOOKS

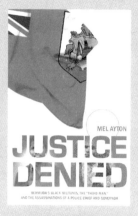

**JUSTICE DENIED**
Bermuda's Black Militants, The
"Third Man," and The Assassinations
of A Police Chief and Governor

**GORILLA CONVICT**
The Prison Writings
of Seth Ferranti

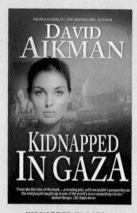

**KIDNAPPED IN GAZA**

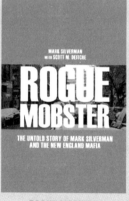

**ROGUE MOBSTER**
The Untold Story of Mark Silverman
and The New England Mafia

## AVAILABLE FROM STRATEGICMEDIABOOKS.COM, AMAZON, AND MAJOR BOOKSTORES NEAR YOU.

## GANGSTERS OF BOSTON
## PRISONER OF DREAMS:
Confessions of a Harlem Drug Dealer